Practicing Love

Journal Edition

A Message of Love, Hope, and Renewal

By Sarah Melland and Deb Bailey

Copyright © 2018 Sarah Melland and Deb Bailey
Published by Ripe Melland Media

All rights reserved. No part of this publication may be reproduced, stored in a retrieval system, or transmitted, in any form or by any means, electronic, mechanical, photocopying, recording, or otherwise, without the prior written permission of the publisher.

ISBN: 978-1-7346333-0-6

Front Cover Design by Sara Mason
www.saramason.wordpress.com

I have decided to stick with love. Hate is too great a burden to bear.
—**Martin Luther King Jr.**

CONTENTS

Introduction 1

Deb's Message 3
Core Beliefs 4
The Awakening 9
Levels of Consciousness 15
Meditation 18

Sarah's Message 27
Be, Do, Have 29
Five Things 31

Law of the Ego 36
Law of Manifestation 44
Law of the Present Moment 48

Part 1: Basic Laws of Life

Law of Free Will 57
Law of Relativity 64
Law of Resistance, Attachment, and Detachment 68
Law of Reflection, Projection, and Perspective 76

Part 2: The Laws of Creation

Law of Patience	87
Law of Attention	94
Law of Intention	99
Law of Abundance and Prosperity	103

Part 3: The Laws of Higher Awareness

Law of Karma	111
Law of Responsibility	118
Law of Forgiveness	121

Part 4: The Laws of Higher Frequency

Law of No Judgement	133
Law of Unconditional Love and Gratitude	139
Law of Oneness	144
Closing Words	148
Meditation Journal	150
References	193

Introduction

Positive and negative emotions cannot occupy the mind at the same time. One or the other must dominate. It is your responsibility to make sure that positive emotions constitute the dominating influence of your mind.
—Napoleon Hill

God, the Divine Consciousness, is the source for all things loving and knowing. This divine source encompasses all life—human and other—and everything that exists on earth and in the vast universe. The energetic vibration we identify as love is the force behind all creation. It is the spark from which all things manifest into our reality based in truth.

It is the connection to understanding who we are and our spiritual purpose in life. Each of us as human beings have the "soul" responsibility for the evolution of that connection. When we understand our world is not created around us but from within us, we can begin to understand how to take control of our own journey and the fulfillment we are so passionate to discover. As humans, we are always searching for the experiences that make us feel successful and appreciated; however, we often feel unfulfilled and incomplete along the way. Each of us, with our own unique gifts, can assist each other in bridging the void between feeling disconnected and being fully aligned with our spiritual selves and the divinity of God.

When we align ourselves with this creative energy, we open ourselves up to the beauty of our experiences and the lessons that present themselves for our own spiritual growth. We are energetic beings who, through the process of conception and birth, have become integrated within a physical body. This energy vibrates within each cell of our bodies, and it is the life force that sustains us. As our consciousness begins to recognize this vibration, it expands with intensity, and it becomes clear that we are more than our physical selves. We are an energetic field that expands out into the universe and is part of a greater consciousness that connects all forms of life to one another. There is no separation—only the illusion that we are individuals on separate paths to enlightenment. We are a collective of souls intertwined with one another, always communicating within that universal web of energy. We can experience this connection when we recognize what it is. For example, you think of a friend you haven't seen for a long time, and then out of the blue, they call, or you run into them. This is often passed off as coincidence or intuition, but in reality, it is the communication occurring through our energetic connection to that individual. Our thoughts are always communicating, regardless of the intention, positive or negative. When we use this collective consciousness for change, we see life-altering events in our own lives and around the world.

Divine energy is vibration that is constantly shifting and creating our world through our thoughts and emotions. Enlightenment is simply the process of raising our vibration. As we do, truth becomes transparent, and we are able to connect with infinite possibilities. Humanity is struggling to rise above the lower vibration of fear, which keeps us in a constant state of chaos and struggle. There is so much pain and suffering in the world today, but there is also joy and beauty. Ask yourself: Do I feel more fulfilled when I'm feeling joy or fear? It is possible to use our joy as an energetic force for change in our lives. The path to personal and spiritual enlightenment is obtained by consciously raising our vibration to that of unconditional love, freeing ourselves of fear and negativity. Understanding the principles of this universal energy we are all a part of can assist us in creating a new path where we experience love and understanding, both of ourselves and our fellow citizens.

Christ Consciousness is the message of unconditional love and service to others—the message shared by all major religions. This book is not about religion; it is about experiencing a more intimate relationship with God, the energetic force in all things. This book is a message of love and hope for a brighter future for all of humanity. It is not intended to provide all the answers to the multifaceted question of understanding. It is intended to open new channels of thought for those who seek more balance and peace in their lives. When we question, we create new opportunities to learn, raising our consciousness and our vibration, fostering self-actualization. It is our hope that the information in this book will resonate with each of you on some level. We are all on a spiritual journey, and the path to enlightenment is a personal experience for each of us. The gift of free will gives us the choice to direct that journey as we choose without judgement or restraint. It is the divine awakening in all of us.

Practicing Love will help you meditate with ease, turn your mind off to distractions, and open your world of possibilities with easy tips you can incorporate into your everyday busy life. It goes into depth about how the ego makes you operate out of fear and shows you how to turn that negative mindset into one that empowers you to conquer obstacles by getting out of your comfort zone.

It goes through simple descriptions of all the universal laws that will help you live a more positive, happy, and fulfilled life. It gives you hundreds of affirmations you can recite when you are feeling down in any scenario. It will also show you which words you need to eliminate from your vocabulary immediately and how to start talking in manifestation mode 24/7. It has tons of exercises to help you live in the present moment, become more patient, support yourself in forgiving yourself and others, become less selfish, not react out of judgement, and finally, to always feel unconditionally loved.

Deb's Message

The path to enlightenment resonates with the vibration of love.

I married in 1979 and gave birth to four amazing children over the next twelve years. We were grateful they were healthy, and we had the financial means to support them. I had no idea how challenging marriage and parenting would be. I felt such an enormous responsibility to raise children who are loving, kind, and intellectually challenged and who possess a positive image of themselves. This is even more difficult in the world today, with so many negative influences coming in and out of their lives. It was easier when they were very young, as I had more control over their exposure to the outer world. As a social worker, I often felt drained and at times ineffective, despite my commitment to others. Every ounce of my energy went into those aspects of my life, leaving little time to think about my own needs. This is especially true for most women who try to balance some or all the responsibilities of motherhood, career, community, and personal relationships.

Although I view the world through the eyes of a woman, I know men also experience similar stress and often get distracted from the goals they once had. Passion gets replaced with living in survival mode in an attempt to meet their own basic needs and those of their families. I would discover this preoccupation with struggle is intended to distract us from discovering our true potential as spiritual beings.

Despite having a deep love for God, I often felt disconnected and alone. I knew God was always present in my life, and my faith supported me through my struggles. However, I wanted more from that relationship. I wanted to feel connected to God's energy, not just know it was there. It would take a mental health crisis to expose my vulnerabilities and move me toward a path of self-healing and finding that connection with God I was looking for.

Core Beliefs

Our core beliefs are at the very center of who we are, what we believe about ourselves, what we think of others, and how we feel about life as a whole.
—Aletheia Luna

We are living in a time of fear of the unknown regarding the survival of our human race and the world we experience. This fear is propelling us into our own state of darkness instead of light and hope we can infuse into our hearts and minds. The experiences shared are intended to challenge and encourage individuals to open their hearts and minds to new possibilities of hope and reflection about the world we create with our thoughts and emotions. We are in a time of great awakening being experienced all over the world as our current belief systems become shattered by advancing research and historical data that is raising the consciousness of humanity.

My journey has brought me to a place of peace, healing, and an acceptance of the divine gifts God has bestowed on me—precious gifts that forty years ago were viewed as unnatural and taboo in many social and religious communities. These beliefs are changing as the world awakens and souls search for information and guidance specific to their own personal journeys.

As part of one Divine Consciousness, we all share this journey, and we will find our way together through love and service to each other. I have been communicating through this Divine Consciousness for almost thirty years, bringing clarity to my own life and the lives of others. Through the gift of clairvoyance, communication through the exchange of thought, and meditation practices, I open myself and others to knowledge, healing, and a greater sense of inner peace. I am blessed with the ability to communicate with souls who are in different stages of their own growth and development. Many of these individuals have left the physical world, while others are still experiencing life within their physical bodies. This is possible by connecting with that part of the self that functions separately from our conscious minds. This thought energy is a part of the Divine Consciousness. Loved ones, spiritual guides and teachers, ascended masters, and other celestial beings are only a few of the many who are anxious to communicate with us.

Connecting to this divine energy allows individuals to fully experience and understand the messages they wish to pass along. Each affirmation brings us closer to discovering God's life force within and our divine purpose in life. Everyone has the ability to communicate with spirit, as we are all connected to the matrix of energy we call God, the source. All we need is loving intent and the desire to discover what is within each of us and what we may not be able to experience with our limited vision of our world.

When I first recognized the truth of what was happening in the world around me, who I was, and where I come from, I fought to make sense of it all. Disbelief and fear were overwhelming as my ego tried to keep me submissive to my narrow view of the earth, the cosmos, religion, and, most of all, my connection to God. I felt like I was in a science fiction movie, and it was difficult to wrap my mind around it. I understand this is how many of you are going to experience this information as you become more aware, and everything you thought you knew about your belief system may be turned upside down. I believe as human and spiritual beings we are obligated to ourselves and each other to question and explore information that can raise our individual and collective consciousnesses. We can effect positive change through our thoughts and actions. The only way out of the illusion our minds have created is together, in a unified force of love and truth.

As pieces of knowledge and understanding fit together for me like a giant puzzle, I felt God, the divine energy, pushing me to remember more, to question and search for the pieces of the puzzle that would fill in the gaps. Why am I in this reality, and what role might I have in transforming how well we relate to one another and view the world? Although incredibly important, just having a good heart and being kind to others wasn't enough for me. I rarely felt fulfilled emotionally or spiritually despite my years working with people in a profession in which much of my energy went to helping others. I knew there was a cosmic plan of enlightenment in place, and I desperately wanted to understand it. I spent most of my adulthood waiting for "the sign"—that one moment when I would know my life in this reality would begin to align with a higher purpose.

I was exposed to five core beliefs in the 1970s and '80s: beliefs I still hold today. None of them conflict with my Christian views—quite the opposite. I believe they bring more clarity to the principle that we are cocreators with the life force we call God. When I was in college in the late '70s, a friend gave me a copy of a magazine called *Connecting Link*, and it would be my first introduction to ideas that were new and challenged my belief system. At the time, these ideas were considered "New Age" beliefs; however, somewhere deep inside, they resonated with my soul. They didn't conflict with my religious values; they expanded them by broadening my understanding and opening new doors in the years to come.

For the next twenty years, I would discover not only that didn't people understand these concepts but also that they didn't want to discuss them. Judgement from others would be harsh, and I often felt isolated. I learned to compartmentalize the information and go on with my life until a time of advancing consciousness. If we are to believe we are all creations of God, then we must understand our connection to that divine love. Jesus Christ and others brought to earth the message of unconditional love as an intervention for mankind. That simple message is the root of Christianity and other world religions, and it is the path to enlightenment and a new world view.

The first core belief is that we are living within an illusion, a false reality we believe we are experiencing outside ourselves. This illusion is created on a mass consciousness level as well as in our individual lives. It manifests in our thoughts and emotions. The systematic manipulation of our thoughts and beliefs throughout history has led to the enslavement of our minds to a corrupt agenda. We are indoctrinated into an illusion that begins the minute we are born and lasts until our physical death, an illusion that deceives by producing a false perception of our reality. This indoctrination creates a narrow view of our world and ourselves, and it is reinforced throughout our entire lives through our education system, the media, religion, and the social and financial limitations we experience. This pattern repeats itself over and over again through the generations as we procreate within the illusion.

The illusion serves as a prison that keeps us bound to a false perception of our true nature, which is of spirit. We are literally creating a play in our minds, and we are the main characters within that production without even realizing it. Every day, we get up and go about the same routines, often asking ourselves "Is this all there is? There must be more to life than what I am experiencing." What we are experiencing is the lie that we are only our physical bodies controlled by our minds. I am here to encourage you to be open to the realization that we are going to evolve beyond the lie to a reality of unconditional love, joy, self- fulfillment, wisdom, and truth. The emergence from an illusion of control and dominance to an awakening of infinite possibilities is within our grasp. We are in a time of accelerated enlightenment, a time of spiritual evolution that is gaining momentum worldwide.

I believe there are two manifestations of the illusion we call reality: love-based manifestation and fear-based manifestation. When we create energetically with love, we create abundance, love of self, fulfillment, creativity, joy, peace of mind, and, most importantly, truth. When we allow our energy to create through fear, we create a sense of lack, resentment, emptiness, self-hatred, feelings of guilt, and a distortion of the truth, which is that we are of spirit and created from divine love. If you have a pessimistic view of the world, you will experience that in your life. What you think is what you get, and these negative thoughts and emotions can become trapped in the physical body, creating illness. They accumulate over time as more and more negative energy and stress affect healthy cellular function. From youth, fear begins to take hold of our lives, and as we enter adulthood, we already have a fear-based perspective of the world. That perspective affects every aspect of our lives, our relationships, and our view of ourselves. Generally, fear is learned through our experiences as human beings, starting at birth. Traumatic experiences in youth are carried with an individual into their adulthood and affect how they view the world.

Trauma means different things to different people. It is constructed through experience and one's reaction to it. Trauma for one individual may not seem significant to another, but it can produce lifelong fears. Despite our positive experiences, I believe we are programmed to focus on and internalize those negative experiences that create chaos in our lives. This programming reinforces the illusion that imprisons our minds. In my own life, I have tried to concentrate on living according to the principles of love and creating a higher vibration. However, when I stepped back and took a good look, I realized fear was a significant factor in my life: fear of not being loved and accepted by others, fear for my children's safety, fear of failing at my marriage, fear of illness, fear of not making enough money, fear of failure in my personal accomplishments, and so on. My fear would eventually give way to understanding that every experience happens for a higher purpose and my journey through life would involve learning from those experiences.

The second core belief is that all forms of life, human and other, are connected to one another and God through a web of energy, a divine cocreative matrix. Whether you call it the Holy Spirit, Divine Source, or the Light or you refer to it as an energy grid, it is in constant vibration with all things. There is no separation from the Creator or from each other; that is another aspect of the manufactured illusion. All thoughts and emotions are vibrations that resonate with the universal energy. Emotions affect our thoughts, which energetically create our view of reality. Positive thoughts and emotions vibrate at a higher rate of speed than negative thoughts and emotions. We are not only physical beings; we are also spiritual beings with energy bodies that vibrate at a higher rate than our physical bodies. The slower the vibration, the denser and more third-dimensional our reality is.

This third-dimensional reality has us believing we are separated from God, disconnected from the truth that we are one with that creative source. Love vibrates at the highest level, and fear vibrates at the lowest level. That is the message Jesus and other spiritual leaders associated with many religions brought to humanity. The goal is for our spirit energy to vibrate at the highest possible level we can attain, thus becoming closer in alignment with divine love. Love and service to others is our path to enlightenment and regaining our spiritual connection with God.

The third core belief is that we are not alone in the universe. The idea that within the multiverses our planet is the only one that sustains life, human or other, was implausible to me. Even as a child, I believed that was selling God short, and as I looked into the sky, like so many others, I thought there must be something more to our relationship with the universe. The thought there may be intelligent life on other planets in other star systems didn't take away from our uniqueness in my mind; it was a testament to God's infinite love and creation. This curiosity opened up more questions than answers for me back in the '80s, and it would be decades before I would get validation for these questions. What kind of life is out there? Is it intelligent life? Are there other human forms of life? How advanced is their technology, and have they visited Earth before? Would their intentions be positive or negative toward our civilization?

The fourth core belief is in the cycle of experience called reincarnation, a process of the energetic soul leaving the body upon death and, in time, having the opportunity to join the human experience again through rebirth. The belief that a soul has one (sometimes very short) human life to find the divinity of God never made sense to me. It seemed as if we were being set up to fail miserably. What about those individuals who were born into abuse and poverty, or those who lacked exposure to religious and spiritual teachings, or people who experienced the oppression of positive personal growth in one lifetime? Should they be judged and denied an eternal life of joy? The idea of reincarnation resonated with me immediately, as truth and its origin in Christianity goes back thousands of years. Over the past thirty years, during meditation, I have spoken to many souls who have crossed over into the spiritual dimension we are unable to see with our limited spectrum of vision. They talk about a life of experiences that continues without the confines of the physical body. Each of them is at their own developmental stage of spiritual growth, and through free will, they can choose to reenter the physical dimension to continue their path to enlightenment.

This ties in to my fifth core belief: that our Creator resonates with pure love. Judgment and punishment are human qualities we have attached to our idea of God over thousands of years. I can't accept that God watches us struggle day to day with all our imperfections and lack of understanding and then bestows punishment upon us when we fail. The support for the idea of a vengeful God seems to center around the idea that human beings will not conduct themselves in a Godlike manner if there is no threat of punishment. I don't find this to be a valid argument. There are so many who believe the tragedies that happen to people are punishment from God rather than the possibility we have created these scenarios ourselves through the process of reincarnation. This process propels us along our journey of personal growth as human and spiritual beings. It supports the idea of free will and the understanding that we control our spiritual destiny and are not manipulated by the fear of our Creator.

I believe experiencing painful and traumatic situations can make us more sensitive to our own needs and the needs of others, opening us to a place of conscious and spiritual healing. In my view, religions continue to practice the indoctrination of their followers, perpetuating the concept of a vindictive and punishing God in order to control thoughts and behavior. This does not resonate with truth about the Creator, who resonates pure loving energy. Control over what we believe keeps us subservient to the institutions rather than encouraging us to go within ourselves, where we can discover our personal connection to God. Prayer, reflection, and meditation can open channels that allow spirit to communicate with us. One does not need to be a theologian to understand and follow the teachings of Christianity, Buddhism, Hinduism, Islam and Judaism which are love, compassion, and service to others. I believe there is power in worshipping as a community personally and spiritually. Coming together to share thoughts and beliefs can expand our understanding and strengthen faith. I suggest there needs to be reform of religious institutions, encouraging a more personal path to spirituality through an equal exchange of thoughts and ideas among their members as well as their leaders.

The Awakening

True progress comes not through action, but through awakening.
—Alan Cohen

When I was in my early thirties, I had a mental health breakdown that led to my diagnosis and treatment for generalized anxiety and panic disorder. My thoughts had become more negative and my behavior more agitated. I could not eat or sleep, and I barely had the energy to function as a parent or in my job. I thought I was dying, that I had a physical illness. The usual testing did not give me any answers as my health declined. The phrase "crawling out of my skin" became all too real to me, a sensation that is difficult to describe to those who haven't experienced it. I didn't even consider anxiety or depression. I always thought I was good at coping; after all, I was raising three young children at the time, working, and living my life. I was managing—until I wasn't any more.

Prayer has always been a part of my daily life, and I was guided to a doctor who diagnosed my anxiety immediately. I was told it was my genetic weak link. Within weeks, I began to experience relief and eventually resumed a sense of normalcy. Medication controlled my symptoms, but I made multiple attempts to discontinue taking it. However, my symptoms would return. Anxiety was always there, under the surface. Even though I had a basic understanding of what I needed to do to succeed and feel fulfilled, I often felt stuck and unmotivated. There are millions of people who suffer from these disorders and many others. This truly is the human condition, and it is pervasive in our society and many others.

When I took a closer look at my life, I realized the many life changes that had been taking place at that time. My husband and I had decided to move from our hometown to pursue career opportunities. We left a community of friends and family and relocated to a place where we no longer had a close support system. We secured new jobs, housing, and found a new school for our two older children. Within a year, I discovered I was pregnant with our third child. It was a very challenging time, and without a support system, I felt lonely and eventually became resentful of the move. Within two years, we decided to move back to our hometown, where we went through the process of reintegrating into the community. Shortly after this, I began to experience problems with my mental health. This health crisis would be the catalyst for exploring alternative ways to cope with my stress and manage the symptoms of my anxiety. Meditation would become my place of solace and so much more.

With time, I learned meditation is not the experience: love is the experience, and meditation is the process—a process that initially brought more frustration than relaxation. Trying to find a time when the house wasn't in chaos was challenging. By the time I was thirty-five, I had four children, a full-time job, and countless other responsibilities competing for my time and attention. I would try to relax and meditate in the tub, only to have a child banging at the door. My relaxation attempts often ended with the dog barking or the kids making noise, so I decided to meditate at night, when the kids were in bed and the house had calmed down. However, at the end of the day, I was exhausted, and I would fall asleep during my meditation. Clearly, opportunity was working against me. During those years of raising a young family, I tried to find as many opportunities as possible to relax. Even thirty minutes became precious to me. Despite the frustrations, I continued to experience an inner desire to pursue the path I had started. I was on my own, with no outside guidance or coaching.

All I knew about meditation was I needed to find a way to disconnect from my rambling thoughts and create a quiet place in my mind. This became one of my biggest challenges—to stop the chatter that consumed my life every waking moment. I would put on my meditation CD and close my eyes, and an assault of thoughts would overwhelm me. *What am I having for dinner?* Thoughts about work, grocery shopping, schoolwork, etc.—they just didn't stop. I finally figured out that along with listening to my favorite relaxing music, I could regulate my breathing to slow and steady breaths, helping me concentrate and facilitate a state of relaxation. It took practice and determination, but slowly, I could block out more of the distracting mental chatter. I could close my eyes and begin to find small glimpses of my inner world.

Reflection and prayer began to fill the space the chatter once occupied. I used these moments of silence to express my love and gratitude for the positive things in my life. My mind somehow found a way to focus on the negative around me, but when I went into my inner world, it slowly began to change, and I could concentrate on the feelings that love and gratitude inspired in me.

One by one, I would think about my blessings and the joy they brought to my heart—joy my chaotic lifestyle kept hidden from me. I loved my family and close friends, and at times I felt joyful. However, this inner reflection was personal: it came from within me, not outside of me, and it was an experience I could build on within my inner peace. The more love and joy I could experience in meditation, the more relaxed my mind and body became. I visualized white light around me and then emanating from within me, bathing me in love and protection. I came to recognize this light as spirit. Meditation became something I looked forward to instead of a chore I had to fit into my busy life. The more time I spent practicing, the easier it became to block out environmental noises that at one time had been very distracting. If my mind wandered, I could now pull it back into the silence.

I would start my meditation with prayer, reflection, and whatever I felt grateful for, and I would concentrate on holding feelings of love and joy as long as I could. I realized that amazing vibration was the key to my health as it resonated within every cell of my body. At times, my body felt as if it could float away and take my burdens with it. With time, I noticed my external world changing as well. As a social worker, I had more energy and patience to give to those who needed my assistance. At the end of the day, I noticed I didn't feel as drained as I had in the past, spending my day helping others resolve their problems. I began to transfer that inner vibration of love and joy to individuals and situations in my outer world. I wasn't just performing kind acts; I was living in the joy of those acts, and it became a source of renewal. Human beings can feel the difference between giving and giving with the heart. We are energetic beings who resonate with the intention of others. Intention is energy, and all energy has a vibration—that was becoming very clear to me. The more love and joy that resonated within and around me, the more positively others responded, and my life became more fulfilling. I began bringing others into my meditations. I pictured them in my mind and would wrap that light around them, asking spirit to send love and healing to them. These visualizations enhanced my intentions of prayer, giving me a greater sense of involvement. I was *practicing love*, and it was transforming. I believe miracles are simply unconditional expressions of love. As I dedicated that love more fully to my life and others, I became more invested in the process of self-discovery.

Meditation started out being a way to relax and improve my health. However, there came a time when I experienced an inner drive to push beyond the darkness behind my closed eyes. I knew there was more on the other side of that veil that I was able to access, but I just didn't know how. No amount of concentration broke through the barrier. However, I continued to direct my intention and prayed for answers. I felt protected by the light of spirit. However, there was an element of fear of the unknown. My answer finally came during one meditation when the thought "Look for the center" came to me. I had no idea what that meant, but the message was strong and direct. Not long after this, I had a vision in my mind of a center, a modern-looking building made of glass. The idea of a center for higher learning seemed to come to me when I envisioned this building. I now understood what the "center" was, but how was I supposed to get there? By this time, I was able to go deep within myself and totally disconnect from the environment around me. I could be indoors or outdoors, and at times, I preferred to focus and relax with my eyes open, especially when in nature. I was ready for the next step, but did my higher self, my soul, believe I was? There is no doubt in my mind there was a higher power nudging me forward and preparing me for each step along my journey. I realized that power knew me intimately and would give me answers when I was spiritually ready to receive them.

I still remember the moment my journey shifted. I took a risk and pictured myself in front of this amazing glass building. I walked up the steps to the front doors, which opened automatically, welcoming me in. I felt anxious but excited to see what was inside. I walked into the lobby and looked around, taking in the beauty, when a woman approached me. She was dressed in a garment that appeared to be linen, and it had a loose hood covering her hair. She welcomed me and told me her name was Mary. Her spirit was so kind and loving that I immediately felt at ease. At first, I was sure I must be imagining this experience or manufacturing it in some way. However, I was reacting to, not anticipating, what was happening. It was all new to me, and it would be the beginning of many lessons and experiences. For the next year, Mary would be my teacher and confidant until I was ready for the next phase of my journey.

When I communicated with spiritual beings during meditation over the next twenty years, they would express their concerns for what was occurring in our world. These conversations were supportive, and I believe they were intended to challenge me to recognize how resigned I had become to the way our world systems operate. Like so many people, I didn't like what I was seeing in the world but always felt powerless to effect change. This does produce a state of apathy, and I was asking for personal growth. They were always willing to assist. These enlightened beings recognize the loyalty with which human beings devote their lives to their systems of government, systems that not only serve an elite and powerful few but also have little interest in the preservation of the human condition. This seems derogatory, but from their perspective, it is reflective of the conscious narrative that is so hard to break free from.

For thousands of years, basic human rights have been stripped from mankind, yet the masses remain subservient to this ego-based suppression: not a self-determining system of governing but an ongoing attempt to prop up those who have the most wealth and influence. In part, this is to be expected as most of the population sleepwalks through life. Humans have so little aspiration to rise above the ego and enter into a humanitarian system of living. The good works that are happening around the world get very little attention in the media. Our current system cannot change without an understanding of what makes a society great. It is a struggle that, although difficult, can be achieved. Love and compassion for others are ideals many people believe in. However, they don't seem to bring the satisfaction that wealth and economic personal success bring. Our distorted financial system is drowning people in debt. In theory, this system should be a way of serving everyone; instead, it is easily manipulated to benefit a few. The separation between rich and poor makes it obvious that this system will never serve all equally. People in the West, particularly, have been brainwashed to believe in this system, which has led to the dramatic downfall of our way of life. Any suggestions of alternative systems are met with ridicule and skepticism.

There are other ways to fulfill humans' obligation to each other; however, at this time, these efforts don't seem to have an impact that is beneficial to the whole. It is remarkable how the wealthiest members of society can turn a blind eye to the sick and starving on the planet. Those who truly recognize and have experienced this level of suffering seem powerless to make effective change. Many individuals give to charities with compassionate intention, but this is just a Band-Aid on a bleeding wound—it does not change the core problem in our reality. The layers are complicated and wrapped so tightly around each other, held together by a multifaceted illusion controlled by programming that keeps us ignorant of the truth as a united force of love and cocreative abilities.

Each one of us has the ability to effect change in our world, but this is not what we have been conditioned to believe. We have been subtly and deliberately programmed to believe in struggle, fear, and apathy and to accept dissension among ourselves as normal. We are functioning in a world that is consumed with individualism instead of community. Why is it so difficult to make others our priority when we live in a world that so desperately needs a sense of community, a sense of unity and striving for the common goal of peace and success for all? Our conditioning has us believing that looking out for others does not serve our individual needs. It is imperative that we understand we will continue to destroy our world until we realize the only path to healing humanity is through compassion toward others and building on the idea of community.

Successful civilizations work cooperatively, with the welfare of the whole as their priority. No one is less important than anyone else, and everyone is necessary for making the whole complete. Their leaders prioritize their communities over their own interests. The community as a whole is protected and provided for, and they share an understanding of being a part of something bigger than themselves, a creative process that extends from within and reaches out to effect positive change and build a world of harmony. They practice the belief they are a part of one creative energy not bound by thought. This energy is universal and cannot be manipulated because it is based in truth. We have the ability to effect change in our world, as we are more than what we appear to be. We are spiritual beings who cocreate the world we see, and we are all responsible for effecting change to our reality through positive thought and action. We must wake up from our apathy and center ourselves in love, the vibration of creation. This vibration, when practiced in unison, can change mass consciousness and bring healing to mankind and the planet. Without this intention, we will continue to be enslaved in an illusion of fear and despair. It has always been our choice, and it will continue to be.

Place of Peace

I began my meditation with a prayer of gratitude. I told God I loved him with all my heart and soul. I thanked him for my brothers and sisters on earth and in the celestial realm and expressed my gratitude for the unconditional love I felt. I asked that he help me be worthy of the tasks that may be asked of me and that I remain committed to serving others. I thanked God for the opportunity to serve a greater purpose than myself, something I had been waiting for all my life.

As I prayed, I felt God's incredible love radiate from within me—not around me, but within me. I floated peacefully within the prayer and knew I was loved and protected. I prayed that I would begin to remember my life prior to my incarnation into this reality, a life that I was struggling to remember in my conscious mind. I wasn't interested in a past memory of life on earth but a memory of my true origin. I needed to awaken to the truth of who I am and where my soul comes from.

For much of my adulthood, I never felt I belonged on earth. I had periods of immense loneliness, and I would ask God to let me go home, wherever that was. This had nothing to do with wanting to die; I just wanted God to remove me from this reality. I loved my family, and I knew they loved me, but this was different. Over the years, I have spoken to many who have expressed these same thoughts and feelings—a sense of not belonging.

As I meditated, images began to come to me. I saw a park the size of a city, filled with beautiful lush green gardens. There were plants that seemed somewhat familiar but many I had never seen before. I saw large pools of water that I knew were created to energize and heal the physical and energy bodies. Everything I saw was radiating with light energy. I went further into my meditation and saw a gathering of many beings in a large open cathedral, beings glowing with light and love, praying together, silently connecting with the Creator. These beings were physical and yet highly energetic, like there was a force field around them, a glowing mass of light emanating from them and upward toward the heavens. It was such an amazing experience, and I knew in my heart I had been there before. As I looked around at the absolute serenity and beauty of this place, I couldn't help wishing I could stay forever. It felt so familiar and filled me with joy. I realized I had just made my first trip to a place free from struggle, and for the first time, I was truly at peace.

We are never alone. The beauty of the Creator is everywhere we look. Nature, the universe, and our own bodies all possess incredible mysteries that strengthen the belief that something more powerful than ourselves exists. That divine beauty is woven throughout our lives. Whether we stop to recognize it or not, it is our birthright. The illusion of need in our lives cannot diminish or take that away; it only serves to keep us feeling disconnected. Our very existence appears predicated on the idea that deprivation and fear motivate us to improve our lives when love and gratitude are truly the catalysts for change.

The Light is all around us, surrounding us with grace and love. It is never fading and always there to protect and inspire us. All that is required is that we bring it into our lives. Every day, we struggle with life's challenges, and it is easy to feel isolated and alone. We are never alone.

—*Spirit*

THE LEVELS OF CONSCIOUSNESS

The key to growth is the introduction of higher dimensions of consciousness into our awareness. —Lao Tzu

Manifesting a fulfilling life begins with understanding the role of the conscious, subconscious, and unconscious minds. Although the following information is a very simplistic explanation, I hope it gives you a basic understanding of the very complex process that affects every aspect of our lives. We are complicated human beings with many experiences, both positive and negative, that shape who we are and what we believe about ourselves and the lives we have created.

Our conscious mind, or ego, is responsible for reasoning and logic. It is our connection to the external world and is most associated with our personalities. It is neither positive nor negative, as it makes decisions based on the information available in any given situation and uses that information for the protection and survival of the individual. When the ego feels threatened, it will make decisions to reduce the perceived threat. This is different for every individual based on their own life experiences.

The conscious mind also facilitates our interactions with others and our environment. It keeps us connected to reality and the illusion we call life. It collects information from the environment at a rapid rate, uses what it needs, and sends the rest to the subconscious mind to be utilized at another time if necessary. The conscious mind acts as a mediator between our basic desires and our beliefs and values, which, at times, conflict with one another. We may desire something the conscious mind understands may conflict with our beliefs and values and make decisions accordingly. It must make decisions it perceives are in our best interests.

Practically speaking, the subconscious mind acts as a short-term storage program for many of our behavior patterns and common functions. For example, when you drive to a destination and you can't remember the route you took to get there, it was the subconscious mind carrying out the task while your conscious mind was preoccupied. Within the subconscious mind is where our beliefs develop relative to our experiences. How we are parented, interactions with the education system, religious indoctrination, and relationships all shape our beliefs and values and are stored in the subconscious mind. Some of our beliefs serve us well, and some of them do not. The beliefs we have learned that do not serve us well can subconsciously sabotage our desire to prosper and be happy.

From childhood, the unconscious mind acts as a computer, recording all our experiences and the thoughts and emotions associated with those experiences. Starting at birth, the unconscious mind stores our experiences as memories related to our primal need for survival. This is an unconscious function that continues throughout our lives. The unconscious mind is the storage center for these experiences, which are often buried very deep, far from our conscious reality. It is in the unconscious mind where buried memories of trauma are stored. It is the function of the subconscious mind to retrieve and interpret those experiences when called upon to do so by the conscious mind. Often, unconscious memories are forgotten and difficult to retrieve without professional intervention. We develop many coping mechanisms, attempting to protect ourselves from emotional pain and perceived suffering. It is important to note that trauma is different for everyone. There are few of us who have not experienced painful events we do not consciously want to remember. Although buried, these memories can have a profound impact on the quality of our lives, shattering our trust in ourselves and the world we perceive around us.

We may think we are deserving of happy lives, great jobs, positive relationships, etc.; however, over time, our subconscious minds may have formed the belief that we are not worthy of these things. As much as we try to convince ourselves we are deserving and try to stay positive and focused, we fall short of our desired goals. Being positive, loving, and goal centered is important; however, we must consider the role our subconscious minds may play in limiting our potential.

The higher self is often referred to as the energetic essence, the *soul*. It is our direct connection to the Creator, and all spiritual communication goes through the higher self. When we are fully conscious, we have little awareness of the higher self, and life around us keeps us believing we are disconnected from this aspect of our being. Spiritually speaking, there is no separation: each of us is one mind, body, and soul cocreating our inner and outer worlds.

The higher self always comes from a place of love, peace, and balance—never judgement. It is all loving, knowing, creative, intelligent, and truthful. It is aware of everything we do, always working to guide and support us. It is not influenced by the constantly shifting thoughts and emotions driven by our conscious mind. Making an effort to consciously tune into its existence is the source of our personal and spiritual growth.

It is the higher self that holds the script for all we have set out to achieve in our lifetime. Imagine if we could tap into this plan and discover why we have chosen to experience all the pain and joys of our life experience. How much more effective could we be if we really understood what our real-life plan is?

Now you may consciously believe you have no underlying plan in your life. However, if you review your life closely, you will find certain things happened in your life (you may call them chance or coincidence) that helped or forced you to change directions in ways that were ultimately beneficial for you. Wouldn't it be great to become more aware of the signals we are getting from our higher self? This could help us smooth the transitions brought on by those life events we all seem to face at certain times in our lives.

By understanding how past experiences have shaped our views, we can gain insight into aspects of ourselves we may need to alter to become balanced and effective in our lives. By making adjustments in the ways we think, feel, and behave, we can create a much more positive future for ourselves and others.

The key to moving forward is discovering what beliefs may be holding us back from a life of fulfillment. Self-reflection involves having honest conversations with ourselves about beliefs that are counter to our reaching our goals. These common issues are often barriers to creating a successful life.

Ask yourself:

- Do I believe I am loved?
- Am I a loving person?
- What do I believe about relationships?
- What are my beliefs about parenting?
- What do I believe about my earning potential?
- Am I afraid to fail, and do I believe I deserve to be successful?
- Am I worthy of being happy?
- Am I afraid of judgment from others?
- Do I judge others?
- How are my negative thoughts benefiting me?
- Am I able to forgive myself and others?
- Do I believe my life has to be a struggle?

MEDITATION

The goal of meditation isn't to control your thoughts, it's to stop letting your thoughts control you.
—Author Unknown

Stress is the direct result of our reaction to situations that occur in our lives. The body has an electrical (energetic) frequency that is measurable. Negative thoughts and emotions are not only expressed outwardly but also become internalized as destructive energy patterns. These patterns disrupt the natural flow of energy affecting cells vital to overall health and well-being. Even slight changes in energetic patterns and cellular structures can lead to illness. A great deal of emphasis has been placed on the mental, emotional, and physical benefits of relaxation and meditation. Research has shown increasing and balancing our energetic fields reduces stress and has a positive effect on blood pressure, heart rate, metabolism, blood sugar, cell regeneration, and more.

Studies have concluded our emotions affect our DNA in dramatic ways. The implications are significant to understanding how our emotional state affects our health and overall quality of life. Strands of DNA were exposed to positive and negative emotions in a controlled setting, and the DNA responded uniquely to both. When the participants focused on negative emotions such as fear and anger, the elongated spiral strands knotted up, changing their form and influencing their function. When positive emotions such as love and gratitude were experienced, the DNA became more relaxed and at times appeared more fluid, as if enhancing its intended purpose. Understanding the correlation, it makes sense to ground ourselves in positive thoughts and emotions.

Perhaps if we make a conscious effort to allow more love and gratitude to find its way into our lives, we can change our health and the world we live in. Learning to escape the chaos our world presents to us every day, even for a short time, can reduce the effects of stress on our minds and bodies. Going within ourselves allows us to experience the moment, free from worries about the past and future.

Meditation is a state of reflection, contemplation, and introspection. It is an exploration of each moment in our lives without judgement. Mindful meditation can facilitate this process by consciously accessing the subconscious mind and reconciling current beliefs with those that align with our higher purpose. To find introspection, we need to go within the silence of our inner personal thoughts, deep beyond the conscious reality that is clouding our thoughts and emotions. Everyday chatter in the mind works overtime to keep us preoccupied with the chaos of our daily lives. This chaos serves to keep us separated from discovering who we are and our connection to spirit. When we allow ourselves to transcend consciousness, we open doors to new thoughts and a way out of the old patterns that keep us feeling trapped. These doors open to show us new possibilities and the pursuit of our dreams and aspirations. Connecting to this inner world brings insight and the realization that we are more than our human expectations: we are cocreators with the divine.

Be still and experience the peacefulness that exists in the solitude of quiet. No judgement, pain, or worries, for within the stillness lies the comfort of the Creator's love. An energetic force within that knows each of us intimately waiting to wrap us in the light of glory. An energy capable of healing the mind, body, and soul when attuned to its message.
—*Spirit*

What keeps us from delving into this inner world of stillness? Perhaps the fear of the unknown or our own misguided expectations. We often want immediate gratification and become disillusioned when our expectations fail us. We have become a society that seeks reward from external sources, a material world that promises to make our dreams come true. Why, then, are we suffering from addiction, anxiety, depression, disease, and a loss of self-identity? Our basic needs become our priority. Raising children, working to keep a roof over our heads, and maintaining personal relationships become the focus of our attention and energy. For many, it is times of crisis that force us to reevaluate our priorities and our need for balance. The external world, with all it has to offer, is a source of distraction from discovering ourselves and the beauty and creativity we hold within. We must find a balance between our inner and outer worlds in order to strengthen the quality of our lives.

Altered state of consciousness is a mental state the conscious mind can be aware of, but not in its usual wakeful condition. We all enter states of altered consciousness from time to time. This can occur during illness, hypnosis, hallucinations, meditation, or daydreaming. It happens when we are driving and can't remember parts of the drive or we lose focus on whatever we are engaged in as our minds temporarily wander from the experience. There is no single experience that defines an altered state of mind. A walk, bath, music, or favorite hobby may bring us to a state of relaxation, when we are totally in the moment, free of our daily concerns. This is considered an altered state of experience. These mindful states can broaden our perspective about our lives that the intellect is not able to do. Ironically, we look for answers from the same conscious mind that created our problems in the first place. It is important to think through our problems while at the same time recognizing when they have become self-perpetuating. There are practices that can facilitate a state of relaxation and enhance the ability to shut out the outside world where stress is usually the norm.

Through the process of going within a state of mindfulness, it is possible to connect with our inner truth, free from the influence of our conscious mind. The goal of reflection and introspection is to enter a state of mindfulness, where the chatter of the conscious mind is minimized and often disconnected from the experience. This opens us up to a free flow of information through ideas, visions, sensations, and urges. Although direct conversation through thought occurs, communication is often understood with a language that's different from thought, a sense of knowing that can be transformative. There are many different techniques used to facilitate this process, and they depend on an individual's own preferences and goals. An individual may choose to simply use techniques to relax and quiet the mind or go deeper into an altered state where they can transcend space and time and even travel between dimensions. This is all possible, depending on the skill level achieved through practice, dedication, and determination.

Many of us have become frustrated when our attempts to find peace through some form of meditation have left us feeling unfulfilled. Poor technique, time constraints, and unrealistic expectations have led individuals to abandon the practice. No one becomes a master without some commitment and practice. The following information is intended as a guide to those who are interested in meditation but don't know where to begin and have the misperception that meditation can only be accomplished with expensive lessons or practices they don't feel comfortable with.

Intention is a very powerful energetic force. It transforms our desires when practiced through the energies of love and gratitude. This is how we manifest a more fulfilling life. In the meditative experience, intention is the identification of a desire or action the experience is meant to accomplish: recognizing, focusing, and internalizing a desired outcome. Meditation requires strong intent as well as a belief the intention will carry you into any given experience. Once a desire is identified, a strong mental awareness of that desire is visualized and mentally and emotionally reinforced. Intention-directed meditation is more specific than meditation designed solely to induce relaxation. With relaxation, the desire is to simply let go of external influences and become part of the experience. Both serve a purpose, depending on what an individual wants to accomplish.

Maintaining focus on intent takes discipline and concentration along with a sense of confidence that you have the ability to create change through this process. This comes with practice and experience, as it is easy to become distracted by the events of the day. We are constantly preoccupied with thoughts connected to our daily lives. This internal chatter draws us away from the experience. Many may identify the word "intention" with prayer, a message they wish to communicate to a higher power that brings them hope and strengthens their faith.

- ❖ I want to connect with my soul's purpose.
- ❖ I ask for higher wisdom and truth.
- ❖ I want to experience your love and grace.
- ❖ I ask for healing and guidance.
- ❖ I want a greater sense of peace in my life.
- ❖ I am grateful for my many blessings.
- ❖ I want to learn to forgive and be forgiven.

- ❖ Bring love and joy into my life.
- ❖ Bring prosperity into my life.
- ❖ I ask for healing for the planet and mankind.
- ❖ Bring clarity to my current situation.

How you choose to use intention or prayer within meditation is an individual choice for everyone. You can use structured prayer, have a conversation with the Creator, or just experience the light and love—it doesn't matter. It is the personal connection that is important during meditation. Intention—prayer within an altered state of consciousness—resonates with the divine energy of the Creator.

Visualization allows an individual to deepen and expand their experience during mindful meditation. There are no limits to what your imagination can create to enhance your journey within. Intention, combined with visualization, is very powerful energetically within an altered state of mind. Love, joy, hope, and gratitude are the catalysts for connecting to spirit. This energy transforms your intention into manifestation, without expectations about your conscious reality. Be creative with your visualizations. Allow yourself to understand imagination is relative to each experience and, within meditation, becomes more than fantasy—it is creative energy that connects and inspires.

Light is a powerful spiritual symbol and can be used in many ways. If your intention is for self-healing, you may want to visualize a healing light. Let your intuition guide you. Does it tell you to direct the light within or around your body? Does a specific part of your body come to mind that may need healing? Perhaps the thought of a blue or pink light crosses your mind. Different colors of light have different healing properties within meditation, just as in our conscious reality, where light/color therapy is used to heal. The same principle applies to healing others when using light as an aid within your visions.

There are also many ways to use visualizations for relaxation and guidance. You can picture yourself sitting by a place you find relaxing and beautiful. Water and nature are also powerful spiritual symbols to use during meditation. You could picture yourself by a lake, river, or waterfall. Maybe you want to visualize a favorite place that brings you solace. It could be walking in the woods, sitting in a garden—use your imagination. Be present there and experience the peace it brings you. You can bring loved ones into your meditation within these settings as well. Picture yourself in that setting, sitting with a loved one who has crossed over. Are they trying to communicate with you verbally or with their emotions? It is within this state of spirit connection that you are able to join with a loved one's energy. When you are in an altered state of consciousness, sensations and emotions are heightened and very powerful. They are as real as if they were occurring in your physical reality. Remember, whether you are in a conscious state of mind or an altered state, it is the emotional connection you draw from more than the physical connection.

  Don't be burdened by insecure thoughts telling you don't know what you're doing. There is no right or wrong way to respond to what your intuition communicates to you. This will be easy for some, and for others, it will take practice. The more you become comfortable with visualization, the more creative you will become. Each of us has our own internal guidance directing and preparing us for our spiritual journey. When you are ready, spirit will begin to give you more information and expand your experiences, if that is what your intention is. The only things that limit us are our fear and our egos.

Time Constraints. The more often you practice meditating, the easier it will be to move away from the chatter in your mind to a place of peace and relaxation. With our busy lives, it is often difficult to devote time to meditation. Daily practice is preferred; however, even if you can only set time aside several days a week, you will still receive the benefits. Choose a time of day when you are most relaxed, as it is often difficult to concentrate when you have many issues on your mind. When you are feeling stressed may seem like the appropriate time to meditate. However, individuals become frustrated when they are not successful at shutting out the thoughts of the day. As you become more disciplined at maintaining focus, it will be easier to meditate any time of day. As little as 15–30 minutes of uninterrupted relaxation can have a positive effect on health that lasts for hours. Over time, relaxation has a cumulative effect on the mind and body that provides long-term health benefits.

Expectations. There is no single way to meditate. Everyone has their own preferences and through practice and experience will decide what techniques are most effective for them. Experiences during meditation are varied and unique to every individual. We don't have to sit cross-legged chanting "Om" to reach an altered state of consciousness. Many techniques are unrealistic for individuals who may have physical limitations. We all experience our inner wisdom and how to access it much differently. Going into meditation with expectations for a certain outcome usually leads to disappointment. Be patient with your efforts, and you will begin to shift into a more rewarding experience. Sitting quietly in the moment is successful meditation.

  Whether or not you believe in a higher power or a divine Creator, the benefits of meditation are proven. It transcends age, religion, and societal boundaries. The energy is present and makes no judgements about an individual's lifestyle or belief system.

These are some basic principles that facilitate the state of relaxation:
- ❖ Beginners should try to relax in the same space for each session to become comfortable with the surroundings. This is often called our "sacred space," as it is where we become most vulnerable to our personal insights. That space can be anywhere an individual feel

safe and peaceful, indoors or out. With practice, it will become easier to reflect in almost any setting.

- ❖ The space should be away from unwanted noises. Noise in the environment creates distraction and is one of the biggest obstacles to successful reflection.

- ❖ It is best if there are no large electronic devices in the space, such as computers, tablets, WiFi routers, TVs, etc., as they emit electromagnetic frequencies that can affect the body's energetic field.

- ❖ The temperature in the space should be comfortable—not too warm or too cold. Warmer temperatures can be more conducive to relaxation; for some, however, cooler temperatures are better conductors of energy.

- ❖ Lighting should be natural; bright lighting can be distracting. Many individuals use candlelight as a natural source of illumination if the room is dark. Some may prefer the room to be dim; it is a personal preference.

- ❖ Clothing should be loose fitting and comfortable.

- ❖ It is best to sit in a comfortable chair with your back straight and your feet flat on the floor. It is not necessary to sit cross-legged on the floor; in fact, that position is very uncomfortable for many people. The goal is to eliminate any discomfort, losing awareness of your body and surroundings. This helps to ensure a relaxed transition into the experience.

- ❖ Music can facilitate relaxation. If music is preferred, it should be carefully chosen. It should be free from rhythmic changes, which can be distracting. The rhythm should be slow, steady, and created for meditation. Music should be just loud enough to hear it; it should not be the focus of attention. Music resonates with both the cells in our bodies and our energetic fields.

- ❖ Breathing is essential to relaxing the body and mind. It is important that your breath be slow and rhythmic. Inhale slowly through the nose, and then exhale through the mouth. The sound of your breath as well as the breath itself facilitate an altered state of mind. Individuals are cautioned not to take deep breaths, as deep breathing can cause anxiety in some people. Take normal breaths, which are more conducive to relaxation. Counting breaths is not necessary but can be beneficial as a means of focusing attention and establishing a rhythmic pattern. With regular practice, it will become easier to maintain proper breathing techniques.

- ❖ Guided meditations can be beneficial for relaxation. These audio recordings generally use a calm voice to guide you into a state of relaxation. You can find many guided meditations online and in stores. If your goal is to go deeper within your mind where there is silence, guided meditations might not be for you; they can be distracting and keep you grounded in your conscious reality.

Essential oils are well known for their healing properties. These oils have an energetic vibration, and each specific oil resonates at a different rate, some higher than others. Their natural vibration is what makes them beneficial for an individual's overall health and well-being. The scents of essential oils can facilitate a deeper state of relaxation and promote energetic balance emotionally, mentally, physically, and spiritually. Essential oils can be used individually or in combination according to your individual preference. Listen to your intuition when choosing essential oils. Ask yourself which oils you feel guided to experience. If an oil is displeasing to you, choose another. Using essential oils should be a complement to your meditation. The most common way to use essential oils for meditation is by adding a couple of drops to a diffuser.

Here is a list of higher-vibrating essential oils:
- Rose
- Frankincense
- Sandalwood
- Palo Santo
- Lavender
- Angelica
- Ylang Ylang
- Myrrh
- Juniper
- Sage
- Cedarwood
- Jasmine

Diet also plays an important role in defining ourselves as healthy energetic beings. All plants and minerals are made up of energy, vibration that is specific to its qualities. A high-vibrational diet is necessary as we strive to raise our own vibrational health. Certain foods are more beneficial than others for accomplishing this goal. Like essential oils, some foods have higher vibrations than others. Making changes to your diet can seem overwhelming. I suggest you make changes slowly and in moderation at first. The idea is to avoid setting yourself up for failure.

Here is a list of beneficial foods:
- Organic fruits and vegetables
- Raw nuts, seeds, and legumes
- Fresh herbs
- Dark leafy greens
- Sprouts
- Berries such as strawberries, blueberries, blackberries, and raspberries
- Fish that are known to have lower levels of contaminants, such as wild pacific salmon, sardines, anchovies, farmed rainbow trout, and canned light tuna. Do your research for more options as well as to learn which fish to avoid eating.
- Cold-pressed organic oils, such as olive, sesame, avocado, coconut, and flax oils

Here is a list of foods and products to avoid:
- Processed and fried foods
- Refined sugar
- Canned food
- White and wheat flour
- Meat and animal products
- Artificial sweeteners
- Canola oil
- Soda
- Beverages containing sugar or corn syrup
- Caffeine
- Alcohol

Exercise for Relaxation and Healing. Enter your experience with an open heart. *We connect with spirit through the heart, not the mind.* Leave your ego behind. Let go of all judgements, fear, frustration, self-doubt, etc. Understand your experience will progress as necessary for your own personal growth. Spirit is in tune with each of us intimately. Enter your sacred space free from noise and distractions. Sit in a comfortable position with your spine straight and feet flat on the floor. Let go of all the tension in your body. With eyes closed, clear your mind of all thoughts and awareness of your surroundings. You can concentrate on a simple relaxing image if you're having trouble keeping your mind from wandering. If your mind does wander back to random thoughts, refocus your attention by blocking them and bringing your focus back to your breathing or your image. This takes practice and some persistence. Your mind may wander often at first but will get more disciplined with time.

As you breathe in slowly, feel your breath filling your body with the life force. Listen to the sound of your breath as you inhale and exhale, letting go of your thoughts and emotions. Breathe in and out slowly, being present in the silence. Lose all awareness of your physicality and surroundings. Feel your body relax with each breath you take. Picture the light of the Divine Consciousness filling your mind and body as you inhale. If you are having trouble picturing a light, focus on the sensation that energy brings into your awareness. See it and feel it flow all through your body as it bathes you in love and protection. As you exhale, see the light begin to surround your body and expand outward as it emanates from within you. Know that you are one with the light of spirit. Allow your heart to fill with love and gratitude for this divine connection. Be still and surrender to the moment.

My experiences have led me to a deeper understanding and connectedness to a divine energy that transcends our conscious reality, an energy that is one with everything. There are no boundaries of time and space within this energy—only a sense of peace and knowing and an awareness of eternity. I have learned to view my challenges as opportunities for growth as a wife, mother, sister, daughter, friend, and professional. I am more able to assist others and myself through difficult times because of my struggles. I will continue to learn and grow as a human and spiritual being. At this time in my life, I feel more complete and at peace than I ever have.

Human beings are like uncut diamonds. Each experience, positive and negative, chips at the outer edges and begins to transform the beauty of each facet. Within this beauty lies our true nature just waiting to be revealed. There are no mistakes in life, only new opportunities for another cut to be made to our imperfections.

—*Spirit*

Sarah's Message

Dear Lord, thank you for letting me serve you and for giving me this opportunity to help restore earth. I will to the best of my ability show love, compassion and empathy every day. We will encourage everyone to love not judge. To embody what the beauty of life is. To give and to receive. To be helpful not harmful and to devote our time to the journey that is life.

When is it finally time to change your life around? When do you say "I have finally had enough of being negative, of hating myself, of being depressed and anxious?" When is it finally enough?

My tipping point was probably when the fortieth person had "read" my script and said it wasn't for them but I was an amazing writer and to keep it up. I wondered if I was ever going to get my break. I always tried to think positive, but when you get put down enough times by people who just want to invoke power, you begin to believe it. There was nothing more I wanted in life than to be the most influential female writer of our time. I didn't even care if I had a family, a husband, or whatever. I wanted to be a successful writer first and foremost, and I wasn't going to quit until I got there.

So, what was stopping me? My ego, my negative thought process, my constantly thinking I was not good enough. One day after I asked for a raise, my boss told me everyone complained about me and no one liked me. Clients, coworkers—they all hated my negative attitude.

I went to see an energy healer, and she said I was so blocked that nothing good would ever come to me. I was blocking my own potential because of my negative self-talk. Well, how could it not? Nothing good had ever come to me, or so I thought, which was completely untrue. I just wasn't counting my small blessings in life. I was just looking at the negative and never seeing at the big picture.

When you constantly hear you are negative and all you do is complain, you cry yourself to sleep and even contemplate suicide because you see no way out. I am here to tell you that I am living proof that there is a way out, but it starts with recognizing your ego is taking over and you're not your true authentic self.

I did a hard-core self-help seminar called Mastery in Transformational Training to get out of my pain and into my heart. It might not work for everyone, and I don't want to tell you how to fix your problems, but each and every one of you is special and loved, and you deserve the absolute best in the world. Even if you think no one is there for you and you are unworthy, I am here to tell you that you are. You are worthy, and you are loved.

Soon after this seminar, everyone was telling me how much I glowed and that my mindset had changed. Instead of looking for excuses for why I wasn't succeeding in life, I took matters into my own hands and started publishing my own books and building my social media presence, and I went back to school to finish my bachelor's degree. I began meditating every day and became an attuned Reiki master.

I won't tell you this is easy. I still have doubts and sometimes the occasional breakdown, but out of that comes greater accomplishments I never thought possible. Soon after putting my trust in God and the universal energy, I contracted with a producer to write three screenplays and then got contacted to write an amazing book for a woman who reached out to me after seeing my success on Facebook. It is a constant battle to flip your mindset to positive, especially with negativity all around you. It is constant self-awareness, feedback, and mindfulness that will take you to the next level of manifestation. If you practice love every day, it will become easier. It will soon become a habit because of the happiness it brings. Start with the little exercises that are easy to accomplish. Set very small goals, even as small as reciting an affirmation when you get up or starting your day by saying "I am grateful for this day." There will be lessons that will take you out of your comfort zone and make you angry, but the sooner you realize those are just tests you can conquer, the sooner you will see the clouds lift and the sun shine down upon you.

BE, DO, HAVE

When I was five years old, my mother always told me that happiness was the key to life. When I went to school, they asked me what I wanted to be when I grew up. I wrote down "happy." They told me I didn't understand the assignment, and I told them they didn't understand life.

—John Lennon

Success in any aspect of life always originates with a crystal-clear picture about the results you desire. If you don't understand the goal, it is impossible to tell if you've achieved success. There are three common approaches to trying to get ahead in life. Only one of them actually works.

The *victim* arranges their life in the order *have, do, be*. They say, "When I *have* enough time, money, and support, then I'll *do* what I always wanted. I'll *be* happy and successful." The victim is always waiting for externals to change before they can move ahead in life. Do you play victim to your circumstances? Are you always blaming others for your problems? Are you a "woe is me" person? The externals will never change; you have to overcome them with thought process by changing your internals.

The *worker* is all about *do, have, be*. They say, "The more I *do*, the more I'll *have*. The more I *have*, the happier I'll *be*." Trust me when I say money doesn't buy happiness. I have served millionaires and billionaires, and I will say at least 75% of them were unhappy. When is enough enough? What makes a person successful? Is it money, or is it the love they are surrounded by?

The *winner* orients their life quite differently: *be, do, have*. They say, "It is not what do I need to *have* before I can start, or what work do I need to *do*, but who do I need to *be*? What kind of person would have access to the kind of outcome I want? Then being that kind of person, what would I be doing? And then having will take care of itself."

Most of us think we need to *have* certain material assets so we can finally *do* something important, which will then allow us to *be* what we truly want in life. Wrong—110% wrong! Flip it and reverse it.

Once we are completely clear about what we want and why we want it, the game-changing question is not "What do I need to do?" but "Who do I need to be?"

First, we *be* what we want (peaceful, loving, inspired, abundant, successful, or whatever), then we start *do*ing things from this state of being—and soon we discover what we're doing brings us the things we've always wanted to *have*.

There's nothing wrong with pursuing our goals and dreams with passion. However, when we erroneously think the fulfillment of any specific goal, dream, or accomplishment will give us what we truly want to have in life, we delude ourselves and set ourselves up for failure, disappointment, and pain.

Remembering who and how we're *be*ing in life creates the context for how we think, feel, and act, giving us access to what we're really after. Ask yourself what you're really after when you have all those things. Is it happiness? Acceptance? If it's coming from a place of acceptance, you will never truly be happy. We don't have to suffer and struggle as much as we do. We actually have the capacity to live our lives with a true sense of grace.

Begin by embodying the state of being you will become from the accomplishment of this goal. How will you feel once you accomplish this goal? It's not about "faking it"; it's about authentically personifying the states of being you truly aspire to be in your life.

From this state of being, think about, talk about, and speculate about the kinds of specific actions you might want to explore. Allow yourself to absorb—don't be in a hurry. If you actually allow yourself to come from this empowered state of being, the steps will emerge with ease, and your ability to take them and allow them to work will increase exponentially.

Have fun with this, get support from those around you, talk to people about this, and know you will probably trip and fall many times along the way. This will not happen overnight, so dust yourself off and chuckle at your falls. When we remember this, our life can really take off in a profound and satisfying way.

Be, do, have is definitely the rarest of the three lifestyles and the most abstract, yet it is the only one that works. *Be* love. *Do* love. *Have* love. In the book *How to Win Friends and Influence People*, there is a profound realization that all people want is to feel important, and there are only two ways to feel important: one is love, and one is power. If you don't have love in your life, you invoke your power (control) over people.

I want to be…

- ❖ _____
- ❖ _____
- ❖ _____
- ❖ _____
- ❖ _____

FIVE THINGS

In a mirror is where we find a reflection of our appearances, but in a heart is where we find a reflection of our soul.
—Author Unknown

Before you journey further into this book, delve into what you really want out of this life. Focus on your well-being and not material entities. Make the list described below. Really cogitate about love as you go through. Think about the moments you have cherished the most, and you will see it was never that new car but the feeling of being able to purchase it. It was never about the pay raise you worked extremely hard for but the accomplishment in doing so.

What has made you rise above the circumstances, and what has made you fall below? What has pushed you over the edge, and what has made you change? What are the sacrifices you have made, and what has made those sacrifices worth it?

What are the burdens and limitations you put on yourself? Why have you done so? How are you going to make an effort to break free of these limitations? How will you stop your negative back talk about yourself? The time is now. It will be daunting in the beginning. It will take work, but you will finally get to the mindfulness to change the present and see a more profound outcome. Start slowly. You are not going to change overnight; this will be a peregrination, and a beautiful one, at that.

WHAT ARE FIVE THINGS YOU WANT OUT OF LIFE?

Now is the time to make a list of the five things you want out of life. It can be anything except material things, as those will cloud your way of thinking and bring on an attachment. Do you want more intimate, loving relationships? Do you want to make better connections? Travel outside your comfort zone? Live a healthier lifestyle? Come from a place of love instead of anger?

- ❖ _____
- ❖ _____

- ❖ _____
- ❖ _____
- ❖ _____

What Are Five Things You Want to Change about the Way You View Life?

This one is the most imperative. You bring every view to your consciousness. How do you want your views and perceptions to change after reading this book? How do you want your ways of life to change after reading this book? What types of views will make you feel the happiest and most fulfilled? What views will make you feel the most complete and important?

- ❖ _____
  _____
  _____

- ❖ _____
  _____
  _____

- ❖ _____
  _____
  _____

❖ _____

❖ _____

What Are Five Things that Will Support Your Growth through This Process?

This list could be anything from turning off the television one hour earlier to friends who will catch you when you say negative nonsense. What will help you succeed? What are the minor changes that will help you through this process? Do *not* get too ambitious at first, but make tiny minor steps in the beginning.

❖ _____

❖ _____

❖ _____

❖ _____

❖ _____

Practicing LOVE JOURNAL EDITION

WHAT ARE FIVE THINGS THAT WILL HURT YOUR GROWTH THROUGH THIS PROCESS?

What are your biggest character flaws? What is hindering you from growing into the divine being of love and light you were always meant to be? Is it the negative hell brought on by the world and the rhetoric we hear on the news forced upon us? Is it the friends you should out of your life but feel the need to help? Is it the negative habits your practice, such as smoking, drinking, or drugs? Why do you feel the need to use these vices? List them below and the reasons you turn to them. Most are based on anxiety, fear, and a feeling of unworthiness.

❖ _____

❖ _____

❖ _____

❖ _____

❖ _____

WHAT ARE FIVE THINGS YOU CAN CHANGE INTO A POSITIVE FROM YOUR HURT?

Now that you listed what has hindered you from changing, list them as if they were positive growth experiences. Turn the hurt into a lesson. Why did you need to go through that hurt? What was the positive outcome? If you can't figure out the positive outcome, figure out the lesson, why it was brought forth to you, and how you fought to overcome it. If you haven't fought it, how can you now embrace it and conquer it?

❖ _____

_____

_____

Deb Bailey & Sarah Melland

❖ _____
_____
_____

❖ _____
_____
_____

❖ _____
_____
_____

❖ _____
_____
_____

LAW OF THE EGO

The ego is the single biggest obstruction to the achievement of anything.
—Richard Rose

The ego is the single most destructive thought process in our body. It is through the ego that we feel powerless, unworthy, and unloved. This is where playing the victim is dangerous, self-sabotaging, and catastrophic to your health and happiness.

People with this mindset intentionally look for the injustices in life so they can tout their self-importance with a "poor me" mentality. Self-centered people are constant victims of an uncomfortable emotional state and easily offended by what they perceive others are doing to them. "I can't get out of this rut because someone or something is in my way." Their level of awareness doesn't allow them to analyze the situation and see that the thoughts and actions of others have little, if anything, to do with them directly. When you kick a door, it will come slamming back.

People who operate from the ego are usually in a state of constant comparison. They seek out and critique all aspects of other people to see where they stack up, and most of the time, they're at the opposite end of the spectrum. They try to find value in themselves by comparing instead of trying to be their own unique individual person. The ego is a state of fear. Rise above to know your ego is not real but a false limitation you put on yourself, because we are bred not to fail.

What kind of life experiences do you think people operating from their egos are attracting to themselves? If the universe is always reflecting back to us what we genuinely believe about ourselves, then isn't the person who is a slave to their ego likely to attract unfavorable situations because of a lack of genuine self-worth? If our perspective is distorted by our insecurities constantly repeating "I'm not good enough" or "I can't," then we are unable to see the value that will result in our best and highest good.

Another part of this process is learning to take care of you as a worthy person. That means making healthy lifestyle choices for yourself when it comes to health and fitness: how many hours you work, how much time you spend with loved ones, how much rest you get, and what food you choose to put in your body.

The biggest action you can do for yourself is to stop playing the victim. Just because other people have more material things than you do doesn't mean you are not worthy of those as well. Also, just because they have those material things, it does not necessarily mean they are happy. In your heart, you need to feel worthy. If you don't feel worthy of those material things or accomplishments, you will never see the light of your own happiness.

When we let go of our ego mindset, we see the world for its true potential, and we can have it work for us and not against us. How do we shed our ego, which has been embedded in us since the day we came to be?

The first step to is to monitor your negative self-talk, monitor your doubts, monitor when you say you can't do something, and monitor when you are scared to do something because of your ego—because of fear.

The second step is to break out of your comfort zone and conquer experiences that scare you, that challenge you—things you never thought you could do because you were coming from a place of fear. Go skydiving, travel to a foreign country, attend a networking event by yourself where you don't know anyone, or even simply go to a restaurant alone. Little victories will begin to make the challenges easier. The pit in your stomach will begin to diminish.

The third step is to stop comparing yourself to others. We all have unique attributes that make us different in the most profound and beautiful ways. There is no scale that tells us the correct way to live a perfect life. There is no scale that can say you are or are not creative. No scale will ever be able to measure the person you sought to be in this life and the lessons you chose to learn. Stop the constant back talk. Stop the "I am not good enough" narrative. Shed your ego and step into your heart.

How to Incorporate Change?

We have all been there—the place where our ego takes over our thought process. We have been too scared to ask for a raise, too proud to ask for support, or too entitled to face the obstacles we need to face because we have been taught that certain situations are beneath us. Where have you been challenged in your life, when you decided not to do something because you were too scared or too proud?

Take a step back and ask yourself why you are scared. Why are you too proud? What makes you scared to conquer the endeavor at hand? What is the worst that could possibly happen if you fail? Look at it this way: it is better to fail at something than to never try and always regret your decision.

Here are some simple exercises you can do throughout the day to increase your self-worth.

- ❖ Feel free to repeat phrases such as "I am free of the positive or negative opinions of others. I am my source of validation, and mine is the only opinion that counts about me. I am neither above nor beneath anyone. I am equal to all human beings, and they are equal to me. I treat all persons with equal respect and know I am worthy of respect in return."

- ❖ Even if it's just thirty minutes a day, work fearlessly toward your goal, your passion. No matter what, carve out time. Life won't change unless you are ready for a change, so show the universe what you want by making that small change. It takes twenty-one days to develop a new habit.

- ❖ Repeat this to yourself when you are doubting your abilities: "I am the best me there is ever going to be, and I have something of value to offer the world."

- ❖ Do something every day that challenges you and makes you get out of your comfort zone. Even just smiling at a stranger or, better yet, complimenting them. Write down thirty things that challenge you and you are going to do one a day for the next thirty days.

- ❖ _____
- ❖ _____
- ❖ _____
- ❖ _____
- ❖ _____
- ❖ _____
- ❖ _____
- ❖ _____
- ❖ _____
- ❖ _____
- ❖ _____
- ❖ _____
- ❖ _____
- ❖ _____

- ❖ _____
- ❖ _____
- ❖ _____
- ❖ _____
- ❖ _____
- ❖ _____
- ❖ _____
- ❖ _____
- ❖ _____
- ❖ _____
- ❖ _____
- ❖ _____
- ❖ _____
- ❖ _____
- ❖ _____
- ❖ _____

- ❖ And here's the biggest one of all. Do this for a minute every day: look yourself in the eyes and tell yourself "I love you." Don't laugh. Mean it. Maybe even cock a smile and wink.

There is a direct relationship between attracting positive situations and knowing your self-worth. You can only attract into your life that which you are being. When you know your worth and let go of operating from fear, you will begin to cultivate dreams forgotten because you didn't believe you were good enough to attain them.

Bonus Exercise

The biggest issue with the ego is that you like to think about yourself and how everything affects you. Maybe you don't and you are the supporter type who gets walked over and doesn't have self-respect, but that is for another chapter. This one is about your ego, and with that ego comes a sort of selfishness that needs to be addressed. Here are a few exercises that will help take the selfishness out of your body.

- ❖ Make a goal of putting yourself last in at least three situations this week. Obviously, don't make a habit of this, as you don't want to seem like a pushover. A good balance is key.

- ❖ Put yourself in someone else's shoes. When you are yelling at a waiter/waitress, think about how it would make you feel if you were being talked to like that. It puts everything in perspective very quickly.

- ❖ Practice being humble and modest. I know it's weird to think we aren't the center of the universe, but unfortunately, we are not, and we need to remember we are not more important than anyone else, even though we may have a higher social status. Honestly, who cares?

- ❖ Be a good listener without interrupting. Pay attention, and don't be in your own world all the time.

- ❖ This one is my favorite because I love surprises. Be all about the little surprises. Bring muffins or candies to work for everyone. Take flowers to a friend's house. Whatever you do, make it little but extremely thoughtful. How could you go the extra mile to make someone's day?

- ❖ _____
- ❖ _____
- ❖ _____
- ❖ _____
- ❖ _____
- ❖ _____

- ❖ _____
- ❖ _____
- ❖ _____
- ❖ _____

- ❖ And this one might be the biggest: figure out ways to compromise. I don't need to go into detail—I think it's pretty self-explanatory.

- ❖ Be observant. I think my biggest pet peeve in this day in age is when people aren't paying attention, not seeing their surroundings and how they are affecting other people. Talking on your phone and walking slowly in a crosswalk is an example that comes to mind.

- ❖ Reach out to people without reason just to see how they are doing, not with any agenda.

FIVE THINGS

Oh, the ego, the hardest burden to break. List five times when your ego or pride has gotten in the way of something that could have been great and profound. List when your ego has hindered you. List when your ego has told you "You aren't good enough." List when your ego has told you "You aren't strong enough" or "You don't have the talent. You aren't smart enough. There are better people who are more creative than you." List when your ego puts you down the most. List why you want to tell your ego to shut up. List how you are going to tell your ego to go away.

- ❖ _____
_____

- ❖ _____
_____

- ❖ _____
_____

❖ _____
_____

❖ _____
_____

List why you are finally going to break free of this negative back talk and finally feel inspired, empowered, and ready for anything. This is why you don't need your ego anymore. This is why you are going to start by coming from a place and love and confidence, hard work and resilience. This is your time, and you are ready.

❖ _____
_____

❖ _____
_____

❖ _____
_____

❖ _____
_____

❖ _____
_____

AFFIRMATIONS

1. I am in charge. I now take my own power back.
2. It's only a thought, and a thought can be changed.
3. I claim my power and move beyond all limitations.
4. I am willing to ask for help when I need it.
5. I do not have to prove myself to anyone.
6. I welcome new ideas.
7. I am willing to change.
8. There is always more to learn.
9. It is safe for me to speak up for myself.
10. I am humble, compassionate, and empathetic.

Now it's your turn. Write at least ten positive affirmations about how your ego will no longer restrict your ability to produce a meaningful, loving life. Create affirmations that will no longer allow you to play victim to your circumstances.

❖ _____

❖ _____

❖ _____

❖ _____

❖ _____

❖ _____

❖ _____

❖ _____

❖ _____

❖ _____

LAW OF MANIFESTATION

If you shift your awareness to your being, it will be your ticket to freedom.
—Deepak Chopra

Everything manifests through a thought or an idea. Ideas and experiences create beliefs that, in turn, create your reality. If you are unhappy with the current state you find yourself in, change your behavior and shift your beliefs.

Beliefs can be changed when you recognize those that are not working for you. You begin to reprogram through the process and discover what will create success and harmony in your life to get the optimum results.

There is an unlimited creative power in your mind that, through dedication, awareness, and training, can be the wisdom you need to rise above your karma.

Within physical, mental, and spiritual laws, you can manifest any reality you yearn to experience. In changing your experiences, you must decide what disharmonious behavior you want to eliminate in your life.

This book is not about manifesting material objects or money. This book is about manifesting a different way of being so you will be happy and content with your situation and have the ability to conquer the challenges you face with ease and compassion.

How to Incorporate Change?

This will not be your typical list of how to manifest. There are hundreds upon hundreds of books for that. This book is to assist with those nuances those books don't touch upon—the ones that are crucial for you to actually manifest the life you have always wanted.

- ❖ The first and foremost absolute is to get rid of doubt. If, in the beginning, you want to manifest something but in the back of your mind you are still listening to your ego saying "Yeah, right. That will never happen to you," then you need to figure out a way to shut that voice up and shut it up hard. We have trained our brains to doubt and to doubt constantly, consistently, and concretely. We are unquestionably built up with doubt; we are constipated, stressed, and worried. It is going to be a peel-the-onion process. Layer by layer, we get to strip away that doubt. Whenever doubt or time come into play, silence your mind or recite affirmations.

- Get rid of any and all negative words in your vocabulary. Be mindful of the language you use in cross talk. Some words to be wary of:
    - **Don't** – Puts you in a box. Trigger word. Doesn't give someone the opportunity to think for themselves and makes them fear that they are not allowed to voice their opinion.
    - **Would** – This is a word making you seem unsure of yourself. Not a direct answer. Take a more affirmative approach.
    - **Like** – Is weak. On the level of "would." "I would like to do that," and so on.
    - **Should** – You know what you have to do to get what you want, so do it.
    - **Can't** – Pretty much the most awful word in our vocabulary. Do not ever you limit yourself.
    - **Won't** – Another amazing word of the crap-filled ego.
    - **Just** – This minimizes the power of your statement and paints you as weak.
    - **Hate** – This one better not need to be explained.
    - **Other words and phrases to always avoid:** Ugly, stupid, useless, boring, what if, problem, no, if only, but, someday, why me, I don't know, it's not fair, I'm not, I'll try, I wish I, I have to, no way, I hope, impossible, never, maybe, failure, overwhelmed, I'm confused, I don't get it, I think, etc. Be confident in your word selection.
- Another important factor is clarity. If you want to manifest a million dollars, great! How are you going to do that—win the lottery? Probably not. Make clear your intentions and how you plan to get there. Be as clear and focused as possible.
    - Now let that go. We will go into further detail about attachment in later chapters. If you are attached to this outcome, it will not happen. So let it go, and let the universe come together to bring it to you in the most magical and unforgettable way.
    - Be able to receive. This might sound easy, but it is actually the hardest step because of your negative back talk. Imagine feeling no resistance to deserving and having your dream. Imagine trusting it is possible and that it's already on its way to you right now. Imagine continuously tapping into the feeling and vibration of already having your dream. Imagine not controlling how it will come to you but instead

taking action based on your intuitive guidance. This is what a receiving state looks like. What if you finally realize you are in your dream life? It's your dream—you just don't realize it yet because you are on the journey to fulfillment. Take it in and breathe.

FIVE THINGS

List five things you want to manifest. What have always been your dreams? What have been your passions? Nothing is too big or too small. List them as though they aren't material things but five things you want to accomplish.

- ❖ _____
- ❖ _____
- ❖ _____
- ❖ _____
- ❖ _____

AFFIRMATIONS

1. Every thought I think is creating my future.
2. I welcome miracles into my life.
3. I am confident in my ability to create the life I desire.
4. I trust my inner guidance.
5. I am giving and receiving all that is good and all that I desire.
6. I am constantly striving to raise my vibration through good thoughts, words, and actions.
7. I am making a meaningful contribution to the world and I *am* wonderfully compensated for my contribution.
8. I will attract what I desire.

9. I am worthy of love, abundance, success, happiness, and fulfillment.
10. I make better choices that lead to desired results.

Now it's your turn. Write at least ten affirmations on a piece of paper, and recite them daily. For example, recite "I make an abundance of money" every day. If you can't think of any great manifestation affirmations, use a search engine. Stretch yourself. These exercises aren't meant to be easy; they're meant to get you out of your head. You can even use the list of five things you want to manifest and turn it into an affirmation. I will let you do that, so you are welcome.

- ❖ _____
- ❖ _____
- ❖ _____
- ❖ _____
- ❖ _____
- ❖ _____
- ❖ _____
- ❖ _____
- ❖ _____
- ❖ _____

LAW OF THE PRESENT MOMENT

Time in itself, absolutely, does not exist; it is always relative to some observer or some object. Without a clock, I say "I do not know the time." Without matter, time itself is unknowable. Time is a function of matter, and matter, therefore, is the clock that makes infinity real.
—John Fowles, Áristos

What we refer to as past and future have no reality except in our own mental construction. We are bred to believe that time is of the essence. On the contrary, time does not exist. This will be a hard concept to grasp. The idea of time is a convention of thought, language, and social agreement. In truth, we have only this moment. There should be no worries, no anxiety—just peace in the present moment.

If you begin to think with no worries, it frees your mind of mental blocks. It's when we hold regret about an occurrence in the past that we keep regret alive. When we feel anxiety about the future, we keep anxiety alive. If we have so much to do, more anxiety. Take it one milestone at a time.

Time is an abstract concept. When we practice remembering that the here and now is all we have, our present moments will improve. If you want more clarity, I recommend you read Eckhart Tolle's book *The Power of Now*. Just always remember that we have no problems in the present.

To me, living in the present moment means reflecting and taking life all in at that very moment. Take a deep breath and look at all your amazing surroundings. The biggest joy I have found in the present moment is playing with my semi-adopted dogs. They aren't mine, but where I live, there are dogs, and they even knock on my door. Oh, the life of being a dog—always living in the present moment and always having unconditional love at hand.

HOW TO INCORPORATE CHANGE?

This is going to be a long list. You don't have to use all of them. You can try one out every day to see what works for you. I made such a long list because all we have in this moment is the present. That may sound cliché, but it is completely true. Breaking the habit of worry starts in 3…2…1…

- ❖ Reverse the order in which you do things. Allow yourself to enter a beginner's mindset by reversing the order in which you towel yourself off, get dressed, and put on your socks and shoes in the morning. This will help your mind stay out of its all too common automatic settings and instead help it stay present in the moment of the task.

- ❖ Pay attention to the full experience of walking. Take a moment to focus on the sensations, the small and large movements you make while walking, how objects seem to move past you, the temperature, the wind, etc. I recommend a twenty-minute brisk walk.

- ❖ Pay attention to the full experience of breathing. Focus on the sounds, sensations, smells, etc. What did you hear, sense, or smell that you missed in the past which made you feel joyful?

_____
_____
_____
_____
_____
_____
_____
_____
_____
_____

- ❖ Play the A–Z game. As you walk in an urban area, try to spot all the letters of the alphabet, in order, as you walk. This works with numbers, too; set an arbitrary number and count them in order.

- ❖ Periodically stop and smile. Become aware of the immediate physiological response in your body. Yes, even when people are around. Get out of your ego!

- ❖ Awaken with gratitude. When we begin the day with gratitude, we train our minds to look for the positive rather than focusing on the challenges, frustrations, and slights we have encountered throughout the week. Name at least ten things you're grateful for.

    - ❖ _____
    - ❖ _____
    - ❖ _____
    - ❖ _____
    - ❖ _____
    - ❖ _____
    - ❖ _____

- ❖ _____
- ❖ _____
- ❖ _____

- ❖ Practice shower meditation. For most people, a shower is already part of their morning routine. But when you add a quick meditation session to this ritual, you can focus on practicing deep thinking and creating positive thoughts for the day. Silence your mind and kill two birds with one stone. Boom.

- ❖ Smile in the mirror.

- ❖ Read inspirational content.

- ❖ Set a daily intention.

- ❖ Define three daily goals, then visualize them.

- ❖ Connect with nature. On a busy morning, the only time you might spend outside is the short walk from your house to your car. Numerous studies have shown that spending time in nature can boost your immune system, relieve symptoms of depression and anxiety, improve concentration and creativity, relieve stress, and improve your memory.

- ❖ Complete a ten-minute exercise warm-up. If you don't have time for a full exercise routine in the morning, just devote ten minutes to moving and warming up your body to get your blood and energy flowing. If possible, do this outside—again, killing two birds with one stone. Genius.

- ❖ Declutter one space once a week.

- ❖ Focus on your work's purpose. Approach your work with love and purpose, no matter how challenging, uninspiring, or difficult it might be. Being mindful of the purpose of your work allows you to be more fully engaged with every task you perform.

- ❖ Decrease distractions.

- ❖ Take a digital break. That does not mean stop what you are doing and start perusing social media. It means stop it. I know we all have FOMO sometimes. If you need social media in your life, try to fulfill that need with only ten minutes of social media exposure a day. If it's your job, try to become more efficient with time in that area.

- ❖ Show appreciation.

- ❖ Practice strategic acceptance. This means to accept the way you feel at the moment. Realize it is okay to currently feel like crap. Once you accept your current situation, you can come up with a plan to change it.

- Take a music break. Let's jam out and dance. Take a page from the Rickey Thompson playbook and just dance. If you don't know who he is, I suggest looking him up on Instagram @rickeythompson.

- Practice humility. When you are humble, you ground yourself with enough self-assurance and poise that you don't need to show off, act defensive, or be conceited. When you cultivate humility, you purposefully let go of arrogant behaviors and thoughts that put you in a selfish frame of mind. Working toward humility is a growth experience in which you no longer need to see yourself above others or entitled, nor do you put yourself below them or unworthy.

- Practice a growth mindset. With a growth mindset, you believe change is possible and even necessary. You don't view your failures as the end of the world—you see them as opportunities for learning. You are comfortable with taking risks, and you even seek out calculated risk opportunities.

- Take a laughter recess. Yes, that means start laughing. It produces endorphins, feel-good hormones that make you feel happy.

- Practice a loving-kindness meditation.

- Give yourself a break from television and the horrible news.

- Practice evening gratitude journaling.

- Use aromatherapy.

- Practice guided sleep meditation.

Five Things

List five things you worry about on a consistent basis. Not having enough money. Your health. Your loved ones. Now look at it through the lens of the present moment.

- _____
  _____

- _____
  _____

Practicing LOVE Journal Edition

- ❖ _____

- ❖ _____

- ❖ _____

List why you don't need to worry about those issues right now *in this moment* and why you should be grateful for the present.

- ❖ _____

- ❖ _____

- ❖ _____

- ❖ _____

- ❖ _____

AFFIRMATIONS

1. The point of power is always in the present moment.
2. I am healthy, whole, and complete.
3. I *am* here in the present.
4. Today is a clean slate.
5. I am at peace with what is happening.
6. Today, I am at peace.
7. I release all negative thoughts of the past and all worries about the future.
8. Today is a sacred gift from life.
9. I relax and enjoy the present moment.
10. I make a conscious choice to live in the joyful now every moment of every day.

Guess what time it is? Yep, it's your turn. Write down ten affirmations about how you will live in the present moment and what gift you will cherish every day. You know you love me.

❖ _____
❖ _____
❖ _____
❖ _____
❖ _____
❖ _____
❖ _____
❖ _____
❖ _____
❖ _____

PART 1:
THE BASIC LAWS OF LIFE

LAW OF FREE WILL

Who desires all people to be saved and to come to the knowledge of the truth.
—1 Timothy 2:4

With this law, know you always have free will to mitigate the impact of an event or to transcend it entirely. This will result from how you live your life and the destiny you have experienced. If you give grace and mercy to others, if you are a positive, loving, compassionate being and you have learned the lessons from the past, you can minimize the disharmonious experiences.

You always have free will in how you respond to any situation. We have the right to experience any situation as we see fit, to put our creative energies out into the world in either a positive or negative way. This is ultimately our decision.

No matter what our circumstances, we have the power to choose our direction. Our goal as higher selves is to voluntarily and willingly surrender our egos to be the perfected spirit.

Energy has no judgement. As humans, we assign a quality to it, whether we see it as a negative or positive experience. To some, an experience may seem negative, while others may see the same experience as an opportunity for personal growth. It is in each individual's perspective that judgement occurs. If this is true, then maybe we can start to view our lives as a path, a journey of discovery rather than an experience we feel trapped within.

Each experience that confronts us is an opportunity to expand our consciousness and bring us closer to the truth: that we are fully and freely participating in life to bring us closer to the divine within us. Our human existence guides us along a path of enlightenment that we are free to follow or ignore. It is our choice whether to believe we are part of a divine plan or we are alone and isolated on the journey we call life. All souls born into this experience have done so freely, without coercion or expectations from the Creator.

We appear as a blank canvas, and early on, we use our experiences and relationships to begin to form a portrait of ourselves. Our beliefs and values create a perspective through which we view the world. This worldview drives our intentions and energetically creates our reality. Our likes and dislikes, our prejudices and beliefs about relationships—all come from what we have learned from our environments. We have the ability to change our reality by examining the quality of our belief systems and determining whether they are serving our higher purpose in life. We are always free to direct our own paths, with the ultimate judgement coming from ourselves.

Our brains have been trained to think a certain way about what social interaction does for the soul. We have this need to be accepted by the masses. We want to feel important, to fit in. We act upon this when we engage in cross talk to feel accepted. What a glorious day it will be when we decide to raise each other up instead of cutting each other down!

Imagine you're at work and a coworker starts complaining about your boss, saying the boss is a liar and a cheat. Your colleague goes on about how they deserve a raise and are underpaid because your boss is a slave driver. They keep going on every day, to no avail. You think the same thing. You feel you're in a dead-end job, not making enough money to get out. You attract these types of people who fit your narrative. You attract this, and you also have the chance to fix this narrative in your favor.

There are a few options in this scenario. You can quit, but chances are you are in this situation to learn a lesson that will bring you closer to your ultimate goal. Why do you think you are being treated this way?

When you go on griping every day about your terrible boss, it only attracts what you put out. You don't have the free will to get out. You are trapped. You do, however, have the free will to take yourself out of this situation and stop putting down your boss.

Start by not gossiping. Do not participate in the negative, no matter how much you want to play along and feel accepted. Ask your coworker about their other passions and how you two can incorporate them in the workplace. Ask them what drives them. We need to focus on our drive and not what is holding us back.

How To Incorporate Change?

Every day, we are faced with an infinite number of possibilities, choices, and questions. How will we know which path best fits our needs and brings us closer to true enlightenment? There is only one answer, and it lies within your heart.

Every day, we need to step back and pause for just a moment and ask ourselves if we are doing what we love, what we cherish. If you are in a bad situation or a negative head space, it will be harder to see the clearer path.

Every decision offers you the opportunity to exercise your free will. When you see your mind drifting toward a negative outcome out of fear, you have the ability to let go. Let go of that fear and open yourself up to the rain of hope that showers down upon you. How do you flip the switch?

- ❖ Take a deep breath and focus on the outcome. Focus on how you would like the conversation to go, not how you think it will go. Bring it out of the negative and into the positive.

- Is it worth it? Think carefully about how you're reacting. Why are you getting angry? What lesson does that have for you? How does your free will change the situation?

- What path forces you into a positive mindset? Think of that question first. *Where will I go with my free will to see ultimate potential?*

_____

_____

_____

_____

_____

- What makes you happy? Simple. Direct.

_____

_____

_____

_____

_____

- Don't gossip. You have free will not to participate in the negative. If someone around you is gossiping, ask them questions about why this particular situation or person makes them feel it's okay to talk negatively. Is this being effective or pulling you deeper into a negative headspace? It is always the latter. You have the right to walk away from the situation and not participate. This type of talk does not serve your purpose or the greater good. It has harmful effects, pulling you deeper into the negative. It will keep pulling you further down into a treacherous hole you can't crawl your way out of. You will be in an echo chamber, and you won't see true potential. You will bring your energy down to a low in order to tell yourself that it's okay.

- Smile with your eyes. Instead of staring at your cell phone, perhaps take a minute to look around you. Bring your attention to your eyes, and smile with them. You will find it automatically shifting your state of being.

- Ask "Why?" The next time you decide to do something, stop and ask yourself "Why did I make that decision?" You may discover that you weren't really comfortable with the decision.

- Exercise the power of your choice. Don't like how you are feeling? Be the state of being that you want to be. Step into the feeling. Be it now.

- ❖ Accept responsibility for your happiness. No one else is responsible for how you feel. Take ownership of your life and get out of the blame game.
- ❖ Take yourself out of a negative situation. Take control. Focus on why you are here and what you need to stay positive.

FIVE THINGS

What are five things you blamed others for that you should have taken responsibility for?

- ❖ _____
- ❖ _____
- ❖ _____
- ❖ _____
- ❖ _____

What are you holding onto that you need to let go of?

- ❖ _____

❖ _____

❖ _____

❖ _____

❖ _____

❖ _____

What makes you blame others instead of taking responsibility for your own actions?

❖ _____

❖ _____

❖ _____

❖ _____

❖ _____
  _____

Why do you feel the need to do this, and how can you overcome this in the future?

❖ _____
  _____

❖ _____
  _____

❖ _____
  _____

❖ _____
  _____

❖ _____
  _____

AFFIRMATIONS

1. As I say "yes" to life, life says "yes" to me.
2. I am willing to let go.
3. I am blessed with the gift of free will.
4. I am thankful for the ability to change my life at will.
5. I choose fearlessness, and I practice it.
6. I am free to reach my own conclusions based on my own experiences.

7. My thoughts are under my control.
8. All my thoughts are positive and empowering.
9. Each day, I'm developing new and positive habits.
10. I can do anything.

Yes, my friends, it is already that time. Write ten affirmations that coincide with free will. What adventurous affirmation will you write down today? Write anything of your choosing, because you have the absolute free will to do so. How do you want to inspire yourself today? Get to it! You have the potential to be anything you want to be, because free will gave you that opportunity.

❖ _____

❖ _____

❖ _____

❖ _____

❖ _____

❖ _____

❖ _____

❖ _____

❖ _____

❖ _____

LAW OF RELATIVITY

Nothing is good or bad, big or small, until you relate it to something.
—Jack Canfield

Everything in our physical world is made real only by its relationship or comparison to something else. Light only exists because we compare it to dark. Good can only exist because we compare it to bad. Hot can only exist because we compare it to cold.

Each person receives a series of lessons for the purpose of strengthening their light within. This law also teaches us to compare our problems to others' problems and put them into proper perspective. No matter how bad we perceive our situation, there is always someone who is in a worse position. When you are upset because you don't have enough money to have a night on the town, think of the people who don't have enough money to put roofs over their heads or have no idea when they'll have their next meals. We take what we have for granted instead of being grateful.

In fact, everything in life *just is* until we compare it to something. Nothing in life has any meaning apart from the meaning we give it. It is all in how you look at your situation—the perspective you take and the way you choose to think about the situation. When you focus on good thoughts and energies, more good things will come to you. Likewise, if you focus on how bad your situation is, you will attract more bad situations, like when you can't find your keys, get frustrated, and stub your toe. Murphy's law.

How to Incorporate Change?

This is where we go wrong: when we surround ourselves with a negative atmosphere instead of celebrating with our friends, we create a block from within that is even harder to break. When we want the best for everybody, it will materialize. If you are hoping this will happen overnight, it won't. Do not put limitations or deadlines on yourself. It will bring on pressure and ensure a negative outcome.

The biggest step is being mindful about why you want to compare something to something else. Is there a definitive reason? Why have you been relating these things to each other your whole life? What lesson is there to learn from why you compare these things?

When you compare a "that's not fair" scenario, ask yourself "Why do I think it's not fair, and how could I see it as fair without changing the situation? How can I change this situation in a positive way?"

This will take a lot of practice and accountability. This is not an overnight healing process. It is mindfulness you need to practice every single day. We all have our bad days, but the important thing is how we are able to defeat the bad with the good and minimize the toll it takes on our bodies. Start small with this process and grow over time.

Five Things

Write down five things you compare on a daily basis, and then ask yourself why you decide to compare these situations every day. Does comparing certain situations help or hurt your mindset?

❖ _____
_____

❖ _____
_____

❖ _____
_____

❖ _____
_____

❖ _____
_____

If any of these situations hurt your mindset, how can you switch and compare it to something that will help you have a more positive mindset?

❖ _____

❖ _____

❖ _____

❖ _____

❖ _____

Affirmations

1. I have the perfect living space.
2. My ability to conquer my challenges is limitless.
3. I am full of empowering thoughts from the moment I wake up.
4. I am an open channel for endless creativity and wisdom.
5. I have amazing positive friends and family.
6. I feel confident in my skin.
7. I love myself.
8. I love that others have creativity that's different from mine.
9. I love the diversity around me.
10. I am happy.

Write ten affirmations about how you will only compare your light with something as equal and loving.

- ❖ _____
- ❖ _____
- ❖ _____
- ❖ _____
- ❖ _____
- ❖ _____
- ❖ _____
- ❖ _____
- ❖ _____
- ❖ _____

LAW OF RESISTANCE, ATTACHMENT, AND DETACHMENT

RESISTANCE
Be mindful of your self-talk. They are conversations with the Universe.
—Angie Karan

That which you resist, you draw to you. Resistance is fear. Let go of the fear by encountering it. Change what you can change, but have the wisdom to accept unalterable situations as they are, without wasting mental or physical energy. Do not attempt to change what you cannot change, including people. Out of acceptance comes detachment—the ability to enjoy all the positive aspects of life while allowing the negativity to flow through you without resistance and without affecting you. The more you resist situations instead of facing them head-on, the more those situations will come to you, and they will only intensify in nature.

ATTACHMENT
Attachment is the source of all suffering.
—Buddha

When you are dependent on something or someone to make you feel good or worthy, you are attached to them or it. Whenever you become attached to someone or something in this way, it is possible for you to be manipulated by them or it, and not in a good way. When you are attached to an outcome, that puts a negative connotation on the outcome and brings doubt into your mind. A great example would be checking your phone 24/7 to see if someone has texted you back. Another critical one would be waiting on results from a health test. You can't change the outcome, so don't attach yourself to the denouement.

When we attach to negative energies such as greed, pride, envy, and jealousy, it can tie us with large cords to objects such as houses, cars, jobs, or bank accounts. This is why we use the phrase "the trappings of wealth."

When you are detached—independent of status, finance, or emotional need—you are free and immensely powerful. God wants you to have a beautiful home; however, if you need to live in a beautiful home for security and status, it becomes a trapping, an attachment. Cords tie you to the home until you change your attitude. When you master the law of detachment, you can enjoy a fabulous home, but if it is taken away, it does not affect how you feel about yourself.

Attachment is conditional love. If you need someone to behave in a certain way to love them, that isn't love—it's attachment. Attachment can be dissolved by true love and forgiveness. When you forgive someone and completely let go of what has happened in the past, you free yourself and that person.

There are many forms of attachment. The obvious one is judging our lives according to how successful we are in our careers. We strive and strive to make a certain amount of money, but how much money do we need to show our success? We judge our success by comparing ourselves to others, but we miss when we do this. We set ourselves up for failure and tell ourselves that we are not good enough because they got there faster and with less effort. When you stop attaching yourself to the outcome, you will see the grace and success in the little milestones you accomplish.

Another huge attachment we need to break is with relationships, particularly finding our soulmates or significant others. We cannot put limitations, stipulations, or requirements on others. As much as you want that person to text you back immediately (or at least at some point), accept the situation and let it be. If they are meant to be in your life, they will be. If they are there to teach you a lesson in attachment, they will. Even if you think that person is perfect for you, there may be obvious flaws you don't see that make them not right for you.

Conscious Detachment

He who would be serene and pure needs but one thing, detachment.
—Meister Eckhart

The Law of Conscious Detachment is a complement to the Law of Attraction that aids us in the use of the latter. It states that in order to successfully attract something, you must not become attached to the outcome. If you become emotionally invested in the outcome, you will project emotions of fear and doubt—negative emotions that will actually attract an outcome opposite to what you desire.

Attachment to an outcome will likely prevent that outcome. According to the Law of Attraction, if you live in fear and doubt, you will attract situations worthy of fear and doubt. Consistent with this, the Law of Conscious Detachment tells you that if you live in fear of the outcome of a situation, you will attract the very thing you fear. Therefore, you must give up your attachment to the result and let the universe supply.

Beyond this, the law affirms any desire can be attained through detachment, which is based on the understanding that the universe will provide. Everything we yearn for is already available to us, but by making an emotional investment in any outcome, we inhibit the universe from providing it.

How to Incorporate Change?

Attaching yourself to an outcome is, for me, the hardest law to break. You attach yourself without even understanding why. We all want things so badly that we automatically do it without thinking. Don't fret: there are little exercises to do each day to release attachments.

- ❖ Stop basing the conditions of your happiness on outside factors. If you feel an attachment coming on, as if you're in a constant state of waiting, thank it for coming into your life and believe it will work out the way it is supposed to. Carry on with other things that always make you happy to keep yourself busy.

- ❖ Replace "I have to" with "I get to" or, even better, "I am blessed to." This is a fun little game of mindfulness. Practice with friends and see how many times you get caught saying "I have to." You will be surprised. It will sound weird at first, but then you'll realize how powerful your words are and how they will begin to change your outlook.

- ❖ Put your focus on the journey, not the outcome. The best part of getting to where you want to get is the journey to getting there and seeing how your hard work paid off. Don't rush the outcome, and take it all in for this amazing ride.

- ❖ Accept that some things are out of your control, trust in your higher power. Trust that it will all work out as it should, regardless. We want it how we want it, but the universe might have something better and different that we never thought of. Chances are it is more magical than you could ever imagine.

- ❖ Explore the reasons for your strong emotional reactions. In order to better detach yourself, you should be aware of the reason for your strong reaction. Three reasons why you may be feeling emotional are: you are being highly sensitive; the situation is triggering memories of a painful past event; or you are feeling a loss of control over the situation, which can provoke a lot of anger and frustration.

- ❖ Nix your judgmental emotions. Try to avoid thinking of situations as good or bad and simply see them for what they are. Acknowledge that everything is or can be temporary. If you encounter a minor setback, accept the outcome and move on. There is something better waiting in the wings that you just get to work harder for. Again, everything is a lesson you get to learn, and always thank the universe for the lesson. Thank God for making you stronger. Thank the situation for making you see you can do better and strive harder.

- ❖ Don't be too hard on yourself. Don't put attachments on yourself. Don't set unrealistic goals for yourself. Don't judge yourself based on unrealistic outcomes. Even a small success is a grand success.

- ❖ Find the good in every situation.

- ❖ Practice relaxed awareness. Relaxed awareness is when the mind lets go of its constant preoccupation with attention. You can do this type of meditation for five minutes every day. Let all the good, bad, and strange thoughts flow right through your body. Don't try to change the negative thoughts to positive—just notice them and let them pass. When we try to stop negative thoughts in their tracks, we suppress and avoid them. If we do this, they will keep popping up in our lives.

- ❖ Learn from all parts of your life. Don't just see the good as success and the bad as failure but as lessons you get to learn throughout your journey in this life.

- ❖ Separate from your emotions. Realize your emotions are a separate event that is passing through and they are not a part of you. Remove their power.

- ❖ Find a solution instead of complaining. Don't waste your energy complaining. Instead, work toward a solution.

- ❖ Let beauty in. There are so many things to be grateful for. Take five minutes and look at the scenery outside. Look at how beautifully the sky captivates your eye.

Know all these practices won't happen overnight. The best thing is to practice mindfulness every day. All these exercises will get easier the more you do them. You will find the ones that work best for you.

Five Things

List five things you are resistant to doing and why you have been resisting them. Where has this resistance shown up in your life before? Why do you think that is, and what lessons can you take away from this?

❖ _____

_____

_____

Practicing LOVE JOURNAL EDITION

❖ _____

_____

❖ _____

_____

❖ _____

_____

❖ _____

_____

Now list five ways for each and how you can conquer them.

❖ _____

_____

❖ _____

❖ _____

_____

❖ _____

❖ _____

List five outcomes you have been attached to. How has that hindered you from letting in what should be coming into your life? Why have you wanted the attachments so badly? Why was it so hard to let go? What could come into your life if you finally let go of those attachments?

❖ _____

❖ _____

❖ _____

❖ _____

❖ _____

_____

_____

List five outcomes you can detach yourself from and how you will be able to do this. It is okay to let the universe provide you with the answer, even if it is something different than what you want. It is always going to be something better and something that you could have never imagined.

❖ _____

_____

❖ _____

_____

❖ _____

_____

❖ _____

_____

❖ _____

_____

Affirmations

1. I know that old negative patterns no longer limit me. I let them go with ease.
2. I attract only healthy relationships. I am always treated well.

3. I release the need to replay situations in my mind.
4. I release things that no longer serve me.
5. I no longer resist the lessons I'm learning.
6. I cross all bridges with joy and ease.
7. I release all drama from my life.
8. I cut the cords with negative relationships that no longer serve me for the greater good.
9. I am blessed to have learned lessons from the people who have hurt me.
10. I send love out to the universe for the things I know it will bless me with and then let it be.

Yay! My favorite part of the chapter—affirmation building! Now it is your turn to write ten affirmations. Release your attachments. Release them and bless them. Thank them and know they are no longer necessary on your expedition.

❖ _____
❖ _____
❖ _____
❖ _____
❖ _____
❖ _____
❖ _____
❖ _____
❖ _____
❖ _____

LAW OF REFLECTION, PROJECTION, AND PERSPECTIVE

REFLECTION
Everything is a reflection of your relationship with your inner being.
—Abraham Hicks

This law deals with the traits, both positive and negative, you respond to in others as well as those you recognize in yourself. Before you are quick to judge, know this is a reflection of you as well. That which you admire in others, you see in yourself. That which you resist in others and react to strongly is found within yourself. That which you resist and react to in others is something you are afraid exists in you. That which you resist in yourself, you will dislike in others.

PROJECTION
The best political, social, and spiritual work we can do is to withdraw the projection of our shadow onto others.
—Carl Jung

Simply put, the Law of Projection reveals everything you see outside yourself is but a projection created by you. All the people you love, all the people who irritate you, and everything in between are all brought on and invited by you.

Most people do not realize what is happening in their lives is a direct result of their perceptions, beliefs, expectations, and thinking. Once again, they would prefer to blame the problems in their lives on outer circumstances. It is your thinking that is creating your reality. You decide what you will see before you see it.

All outward appearances in your world begin with your inward conditions. Your state of mind creates your perception of what you will see in your world and projects it out into your reality. Everything in this world is filtered through the eye of the beholder. If you see the world as happy, it is, because that is what is inside you. If you see the world as filled with hostile people, it is, because that is what is inside you. Whatever you are feeling is projected on your screen of reality.

In many cases, if we are focused on the negative, it is usually because there is something we do not want to admit is inside ourselves. Instead, what we often do is rant about the person or situation. They are this and they are that, so we never really have to deal with our own deep-seated feelings, perceptions, and beliefs. We do this because it keeps us safe, and in identifying what we do not like in someone else, we somehow feel better about ourselves. We also do this because we use our past situations and events to define our future.

Everything in this world is a projection of your own creation. What are you going to create? What do you want to project? It is up to you and your inner monologue about what you choose to see.

PERSPECTIVE
Perspective is relative to individual belief.
—Keith Collins

According to the Spiritual Law of Perspective, the lower our vibrational frequency, the slower our perception of time. Time is not linear. If we are bored or unhappy, it seems to us that time slows down. If we are afraid, time seems to stand still. When we are happy, interested, and excited, time flies by. People who engage in low-vibrational activities may find time passes slowly. When people are engaged in high-vibrational activities, time seems to pass by very quickly.

Time is able to be transcended. People who have particular psychic abilities are able to tune in to the past (even past lives) and/or the future. Different mediums are able to tune in to different time frames. When we are dreaming, we are often able to move into different time realities.

Within the Spiritual Law of Perspective, size also depends upon perception. When we are children, everything seems larger than it does once we reach adulthood. An issue or problem we stress about before we sleep can seem quite solvable and manageable in the morning light. The challenge may remain the same, but our perspective of the situation has changed. Why? Because we have had time to calm down and think about it. We have let our mind unwind and take a rest.

Each person handles their challenges differently according to their personal level of consciousness. It all depends upon perspective. There is no judgment; rather, there is the awareness that everyone has a different reality and perspective.

The horrible person can be seen as either a threat or someone who is teaching us lessons. Someone who "pushes our buttons" may be serving us by bringing lessons about unresolved feelings to our attention so they can be dealt with and resolved.

The Spiritual Law of Perspective tells us that each and every person has a human aspect that masks their divine perfection. As humans, we will continue to struggle with our perceptions until we see and acknowledge the divine light in all things and all people.

A perfect example that describes this law is one of the most beautiful short stories in our lifetime, "The Egg" by Andy Weir. This tale takes us on a journey of self-reflection and how we learn to cope with ourselves. The journey you take is always just you. Just you and your reflection. According to the story, time is a continuum, and you keep going back and forth, past to future, until you have been every single person throughout history. Knowing that, what would you have done differently? How would you have treated everyone you've met in your life, knowing they were all you? In reality, every single person is a reflection of you. Even the ones you loathe are you, carrying deep, dark secrets you want no one to figure out. Even the people you wish you were are all reflections of you.

How to Incorporate Change?

So how are you feeling after that culture shock? Will you go through life differently, thinking every person is actually you? The age-old advice to treat people the way you want to be treated has developed a whole new meaning. Let's explore how we can change our negative reflections of ourselves, projecting love and light from the perspective of humbleness.

❖ Make it a habit to start every day without any preconceived scenarios. Don't try to guess how the day is going to go, and just let it be what it will.

❖ Get into the habit of using visualizations to match your affirmations. Spend a few minutes each day mentally reviewing your life as if your dreams have already come true.

❖ Much of what we project into this world is based on our own judgments. The next time you see something in someone else that you do not like, ask yourself the following questions: *Does what I see in others really belong to me? Is my vision clear or clouded by what I want to see?*

❖ Here's a fun game to play with a friend. For two minutes, ask each other "Who are you?" over and over. The exercise is pretty straightforward: one person asks "Who are you?" and the other responds with whatever comes to mind. People will struggle as they have to continue answering who they are. Initially, people share obvious things—their names, jobs, relationships, hobbies, etc. As the exercise progresses, it becomes harder and harder. That's precisely the point—to peel away the multiple layers of our identity. Reflect on the experience. Do you tend to associate your identity with your profession or relationship status? Did any of your responses surprise you? What have you discovered about yourself? Did the exercise remind you of some forgotten or hidden aspects of who you are?

- ❖ Who are you? _____
- ❖ Who are you? _____
- ❖ Who are you? _____
- ❖ Who are you? _____
- ❖ Who are you? _____
- ❖ Who are you? _____
- ❖ Who are you? _____
- ❖ Who are you? _____
- ❖ Who are you? _____
- ❖ Who are you? _____

❖ Albert Ellis's ABC Model is a significant part of his rational-emotive behavior therapy (REBT), a precursor to cognitive behavioral therapy (CBT). The ABC model consists of an *activating event* that triggers your inner dialogue, *beliefs* you form after the event, and the *consequences* of how you feel. This formula will help you understand your responses to stressful situations. People react differently to similar events; the ABC model increases your awareness. The idea is to learn how to turn automatic negative thoughts into positive ones. The ABC model is a very effective way to reflect on our behaviors and adjust how we react, especially to events we cannot control. What we can control is our emotions.

- ❖ What was an activating event in your past that triggers your inner dialogue?

_____
_____
_____

❖ What are the beliefs from that event you carry with you?

_____
_____
_____
_____
_____

❖ What were the consequences of how you felt?

_____
_____
_____
_____
_____

FIVE THINGS

List five things you resist in others that you know deep within yourself you want to change. Are you controlling? When you get upset because someone is lazy and you work your butt off, is it a way of knowing there are some areas in your life you are lazy about or you could work harder at?

❖ _____

_____

❖ _____

_____

❖ _____

_____

- ❖ _____

- ❖ _____

List five things you project onto others or problems you play victim to—the problems you think everyone has but only you are internalizing.

- ❖ _____
- ❖ _____
- ❖ _____
- ❖ _____
- ❖ _____

Then list five things you project as a positive outlook.

- ❖ _____
- ❖ _____
- ❖ _____
- ❖ _____
- ❖ _____

List your top five words that describe who you are.

- ❖ _____
- ❖ _____
- ❖ _____
- ❖ _____
- ❖ _____

Then ask ten people—a mix of friends, family, and work colleagues—to provide their lists of words that describe you. It's critical that people agree to be candid. I suggest they send their words via email or text versus doing it in person. Compare their responses to your own list.

- ❖ _____
- ❖ _____
- ❖ _____
- ❖ _____
- ❖ _____

What are the similarities?

_____

_____

_____

_____

What are the differences?

_____

_____

_____

_____

What surprised you about people's feedback? Why?

_____

_____

_____

_____

How do opinions from family and coworkers differ? What does that tell you about how you behave in different environments?

_____

_____

_____

_____

AFFIRMATIONS

1. I now go beyond other people's fears and limitations.
2. Everyone I encounter today has my best interests at heart.
3. I always work with and for wonderful people. I love my job.
4. I am greeted by love wherever I go.
5. Today, no person, place, or thing can irritate or annoy me. I choose to be at peace.
6. I experience love wherever I go.
7. I release all criticism.
8. I spend time with positive, energetic, and loving people who care about me.
9. I return to the basics of life: forgiveness, courage, gratitude, love, and humor.
10. People's negative attitudes do not affect me, and I will spread joy when I feel they are down.

Let's write affirmations that project love, reflect how much we love and adore ourselves, and offer a loving perspective on how beautiful life can be.

❖ _____

❖ _____

❖ _____

❖ _____

❖ _____

❖ _____

❖ _____

❖ _____

❖ _____

❖ _____

PART 2: THE LAWS OF CREATION

LAW OF PATIENCE

Patience is a virtue.
—William Langland

Patience involves spiritual, mental, and physical thoughts and action. Through patience, we begin to learn about ourselves, measure and test our ideals, use faith, and seek understanding through other qualities in our everyday lives.

Patience allows all other virtues to manifest more profoundly. When we have patience, we know the universe will manifest anything we want at just the right time. Patiently waiting and counting our blessings, feeling grateful for all we have here and now, are the pure joy of our lives.

Patience tests us to see what truly matters. We spend time angry because of certain circumstances that deal with time, and we get impatient, blocking what could be manifesting at this very moment. When we sit patiently and take in the beautiful scenery instead of getting frustrated at the current situation, life will begin to flow more fluidly and show us what is right in the world. Remember, this is a journey, not a hundred-meter dash. There are beautiful nuances waiting on the side as we wait for our destinies.

How to Incorporate Change?

Since I feel the Law of Patience is the absolute hardest law to master, I'm going to give you some extra tender love and care with a few extra steps. Patience, what a bitch! Am I right, or am I right?

- ❖ **Make yourself wait.** Instant gratification may seem like the most feel-good option at the time, but psychological research actually implies the opposite. According to a recent study, waiting for things actually makes us happier in the long run. The only way for us to get into the habit of waiting is to practice. Start with small tasks: put off watching your favorite show until the weekend, or wait a few extra minutes when you want to check social media. You'll soon find that the more patience you practice, the more you start to apply it to other, more irritating situations.

- **Embrace the uncomfortable.** When we experience something outside our comfort zones, we get impatient about the circumstances. We need to become comfortable with the uncomfortable in order to cultivate a little more patience. Learn what the word "uncomfortable" means and embrace it. We are meant to push our limits for the pure gratification of life.

- **Release expectations.** Don't expect other people to act the same way you do. Everyone reacts differently to situations, and you never know what the other person is thinking. It's easy to get impatient by assuming other people can read your mind. Don't do it. Also, just because you do things a certain way, don't expect other people to do things the way you do. They might get there a different way. Don't get impatient with people for being themselves. When you put expectations on people, you risk the chance of being let down.

- **Don't run late or procrastinate.** It's easy to feel impatient when you are running late. Time never goes more slowly than when you need to be somewhere and get stuck in traffic. Don't put too much on your plate. Side note: running late for appointments shows your lack of intimacy. Not sexual intimacy, but intimacy that gives you a strong connection with people. It is your ego distancing itself from making a true connection when you are constantly late. So if you are known to run late, make an effort to be on time or early. Similarly, don't procrastinate. If there is something you have to do, just get it over with. It will cause unnecessary anxiety and put you in a negative mindset of dread. The calm and relaxed mind is a more patient mind, so prioritize what you need to do, and do the most important things first.

- **Just laugh.** When you see yourself getting impatient, instantly start laughing, because the universe is telling you to calm down. Calm down, laugh, and experience joy for being a Turd Ferguson in that moment.

- **Find healthy ways to relieve frustration.** Frustration can build up like steam in a pressure cooker, and if you don't relieve that steam, you'll explode. Find healthy ways to relieve frustration. Punching a pillow, going outside to a place where you're all alone and yelling, exercising, kickboxing—these are just a few examples. Once you get pent-up frustration out of your system, you will feel better.

- **Tally marks.** If you have real problems with patience, start by simply keeping tally marks on a sheet of paper every time you lose your patience. This is one of the most effective and important methods of controlling an impulse—by learning to become more aware of it. Once you become aware of your impulses, you can work out alternative reactions. Once you're mindful of your actions, you can correct them. You will begin to notice your impatience right before it strikes.

❖ **Figure out your triggers**. As you become more aware of losing your patience, pay close attention to the triggers that cause you to lose that patience. When someone cuts you off in traffic? When something particularly irritating happens at work? Certain triggers will occur more frequently than others—these are the ones you should focus on most.

❖ **Figure out what your goal is.** Have you ever found yourself working extremely hard for a goal, but you felt like you were just walking in the dark, like you were just choosing a direction and blindly working that way with no specific goal in mind? If you want to learn how to master patience, one of the first steps is setting a concrete goal. Good goals are SMART: Specific, Measurable, Attainable, Relevant, and Timely. Start by setting small attainable goals and strategize your big feats, making sure you can measure your success.

❖ **Have a Plan B for reaching your goals.** Sometimes Plan A does not work for reaching our goals. Sometimes we find roadblocks in our way. Just because a plan fails does not mean it's the end of the world. You get to find another plan of action that may take you further than your original plan. You only fail if you give up—keep that in mind. I meditate when I feel stuck. That's when another idea comes, and I am back up and running.

❖ **Let go of the things you can't control.** Life is uncontrollable by nature, and that is the best part. Have fun navigating through the uncontrollable. Feel how amazing it is when nothing gets you down. When there's a roadblock, embrace it. One of the keys to mastering patience is knowing there are some things you simply must let go. You are not responsible for other people's choices or reactions. You are only responsible for your own. Telling yourself those two principles can free you from the sense of responsibility for trying to control others. It will lift a huge weight off your shoulders, and you'll find it becomes much easier to be calm and patient. If you find others and their reactions getting in your way, that is reflection based, brought to you as a lesson you need to face head-on. It's not a lesson you should steer away from or get angry about.

❖ **Take time to enjoy the process.** What is life without the glorious process? Make working on your craft feel therapeutic—not a job but a relaxing pastime you love doing. Smile at the inconsistencies and breathe in the journey.

❖ **Practice active listening.** How often do we sit down to talk to someone without really trying to understand what the other person is saying or where they are coming from? Most of the time, when we engage in conversations with people, we are simply waiting for our turn to talk. When you practice active listening, it assists your patience because it helps you understand the other person's viewpoint and where they are coming from. I know we all want to put in our two cents, especially in an argument, but we must wait. This takes practice and mindfulness.

- **Think before you speak.** When you try to learn how to master patience, take the time to think before you speak. Think about how it will sound to the other person, and consider the consequences your words might have later. What will the consequences be? Make it more loving. When you fight fire with fire, the conflagration only doubles in size.

- **Expose yourself to situations in which you have to practice patience.** Patience is a skill, which means it takes practice and time, but anyone can learn it. I need to practice my patience with unruly children at the store. How do you do that?

- **Assess your boundaries.** We should all have personal boundaries. They help to keep us safe, and they're necessary to help those we love. If you find yourself feeling impatient and like you are being unfairly taken advantage of, you may need to stop, assess, and establish your personal boundaries. This happens a lot in the workplace. For example, when you are asked to cover shifts over and over for someone and they don't reciprocate, it is okay to say no. It will work wonders for your mental health.

- **Trust everything will work out in the end.** You're now doing what you can, and you're waiting for the results with patience and confidence. Whenever you feel impatient, take a deep breath and thank the universe.

- **Enjoy the here and now.** You are now doing something to make success possible later on. Moreover, thanks to the enjoyment of the here and now, you never have to wait again.

- **Be thankful.** Sometimes we are so caught up in chasing the next big thing in our lives that we forget to appreciate what we already have: family, partners, opportunities at work. Plus, research has shown practicing gratitude can make us happier and more optimistic, and it can even reduce stress.

- **Take stock.** Being impatient is nothing more than a frugal attempt to squirm your way into the future, into a moment when you are comfortable and happy. The harsh reality is that the only way to get there is to wait—preferably, patiently. You are here, in the present moment. You aren't going anywhere, no matter how much you huff, puff, and stress out.

Once you realize this and accept the situation for what it is, you can focus on making the best of it.

FIVE THINGS

List five things you need to have more patience with. Do you go bonkers when you encounter slow drivers, have to wait in line at the grocery store, and so on?

- ❖ _____
- ❖ _____
- ❖ _____
- ❖ _____
- ❖ _____

Why do you think you are being tested in these ways?

_____
_____
_____
_____
_____

What do you think it is telling you?

_____
_____

Why do you need to slow down?

What are you missing from these experiences?

Affirmations

1. I trust the process of life.
2. Whatever I need to know is revealed to me at exactly the right time.

3. I let go of impatience and trust in God's plan.
4. I now have the patience I admire in others.
5. I am the epitome of patience.
6. I am at peace with where I am in this present moment and find joy with every step.
7. I am patient with myself and others today.
8. I am patient with allowing myself to forgive myself.
9. I am patient with my lack of patience.
10. I remain patient in all areas of my life today.

Now write about how much you love being patient. Write ten great affirmations about why patience blesses you every single day.

❖ _____

❖ _____

❖ _____

❖ _____

❖ _____

❖ _____

❖ _____

❖ _____

❖ _____

❖ _____

LAW OF ATTENTION

What you focus on expands.
—Esther Jno-Charles

Whatever you focus on and give your attention to, whether negative or positive, will manifest in your life. Attention is the focus of your words, thoughts, and actions. Spiritual law ensures an outcome will manifest to the exact degree you give it your attention. Yes, every single thought and conversation with friends matters, even when you really don't feel that way and you're only trying to fit in by gossiping.

Each individual has different expectations. Although people may have similar life situations, each person will hold a different picture of the expected outcome, and each will create a different result. Each person creates their own reality.

We are to pay attention to the hints, signs, symbols, and whispers from the universe in order to be guided along our path. If we are continuously picturing worst-case scenarios and always talking about our fears and worries, we are actively attracting the energy of those fears into our lives.

According to the Spiritual Law of Attention, positive energies are more powerful than negative energies; therefore, when we focus on the positives rather than the negatives, we are much more inclined to draw in and manifest positive outcomes in our lives.

When we hold the positives in our attention and focus, we are able to manifest our dreams, goals, and desires in our lives. Our positive expectations come to fruition when we hold the vision and do the necessary work.

In conclusion, always be mindful when you talk.

How to Incorporate Change?

We have all been there: we wake up in the middle of the night because of something we think is going to happen in the morning. We try and prepare for what we are going to say to take the evil demon down. Our mind keeps going, and we can't sleep, stirring in our own arduous thoughts, becoming angrier and angrier until we know there is no way we can't win. Or is that just me? Maybe it's just me. If you do that, you do need to stop. It's not good for your blood pressure or your health. Focusing on that conversation in a negative way will not make it go the way you want.

- ❖ Retrain your brain by noticing three positive changes per day. Create a practice of noticing three changes a day that have had a positive effect on people's ability to do work. What inventions have made our lives easier?
- ❖ Strengthen your willpower by working on one goal at a time.
- ❖ Exercise at least twenty minutes a day, even if it's just going for a nice walk.
- ❖ Count backward from one hundred to one. This helps clear your mind of negativity. It also helps you focus on what you want to bring into your life. If a negative thought pops up, start again, counting back from one hundred down to one, to release that thought.
- ❖ Stop multitasking. This is a hard one for me because I always have so much to do. The more you multitask, the more it could hurt your ability to stay focused on the task at hand. Don't put too much on your plated. If you do, you might implode.

Five Things

List five things you want to focus your attention on. List those five things as they bring you joy and happiness.

- ❖ _____
- ❖ _____
- ❖ _____
- ❖ _____
- ❖ _____

Are there things you focus your attention on that put you in a bad mood for more than five minutes? Why do you let those things get to you, and how can you flip the switch so they won't irritate you for more than five minutes in the future?

_____

_____

_____

_____

_____

_____

_____

_____

_____

List five fears you focus your attention on, and then list how you are going to conquer those fears, even if you take small baby steps to start.

- ❖ _____
- ❖ _____
- ❖ _____
- ❖ _____
- ❖ _____

List five things you want to positively focus on every day.

- ❖ _____
- ❖ _____
- ❖ _____
- ❖ _____
- ❖ _____

Affirmations

1. Life loves me!
2. I come from the loving space of my heart, and I know that love opens all doors.
3. My life is fabulous every day.
4. What I focus on today will bring me joy, love, compassion, and empathy.
5. I love knowing that whatever I focus my attention on will bring me a lifetime of happiness.
6. When a doubt pops into my head, I let it go with ease.
7. My day has limitless possibilities.
8. I focus on the abundance of time.
9. I stay focused on what I am achieving each and every day.
10. I focus on love today.

Write down ten attentions you want to fill your mind with today.

- ❖ _____
- ❖ _____
- ❖ _____

Practicing LOVE JOURNAL EDITION

- ❖ _____
- ❖ _____
- ❖ _____
- ❖ _____
- ❖ _____
- ❖ _____
- ❖ _____

LAW OF INTENTION

You create your thoughts, your thoughts create your intentions, and your intentions create your reality.
—Wayne Dyer

Make your intentions clear and loving, for if they are not, they will not come with reward.

If you perform an act of kindness with the intention of being recognized for goodness or you have an underlying motive that is not of the higher order, higher rewards will not be forthcoming.

Intention and effort must be of higher vibration to gain or create spiritual accomplishment. If a person makes a promise to another with the intention to keep it but does not follow through with that action, it becomes a lie, a breaking of one's word, and it creates karma.

How to Incorporate Change?

In an article by Deepak Chopra (2012), he put together five ways to help set powerful intentions. They are as follows:

1. **Slip into the gap.** Most of the time, our mind is caught up in thoughts, emotions, and memories. Beyond this noisy internal dialogue is a state of pure awareness that is sometimes referred to as "the gap." One of the most effective tools we have for entering the gap is meditation. Meditation takes you beyond the ego-mind into the silence and stillness of pure consciousness. This is the ideal state in which to plant your seeds of intention.

2. **Release your intentions and desires.** Once you're established in a state of restful awareness, release your intentions and desires. The best time to plant your intentions is during the period after meditation, while your awareness remains centered in the quiet field of all possibilities. After you set an intention, let it go—simply stop thinking about it. Continue this process for a few minutes after your meditation period each day.

3. **Remain centered in a state of restful awareness.** Intention is much more powerful when it comes from a place of contentment than if it arises from a sense of lack or need. Stay centered and refuse to be influenced by other people's doubts or criticisms. Your higher self

knows that everything is all right and will be all right, even without knowing the timing or the details of what will happen.

4. **Detach from the outcome.** We have covered this in previous chapters, and now it is time to put it to work. Relinquish your rigid attachment to a specific result, and live in the wisdom of uncertainty. Attachment is based on fear and insecurity, while detachment is based on the unquestioning belief in the power of your true self. Intend for everything to work out as it should, then let go and allow opportunities and openings to come your way.

5. **Let the universe handle the details.** Your focused intentions set the infinite organizing power of the universe in motion. Trust that infinite organizing power to orchestrate the complete fulfillment of your desires. Don't listen to the voice that says you have to be in charge, that obsessive vigilance is the only way to get anything done. The outcome you try so hard to force may not be as good for you as the one that comes naturally. You have released your intentions into the fertile ground of pure potentiality, and they will bloom when the season is right.

If you are on this journey, I highly recommend Chopra's book, *The Seven Spiritual Laws of Success*.

FIVE THINGS

Write down five intention statements. These statements will be brief, crystal clear, and inspiring. Write as if they are happening now. Focus on the feelings you have, and use positive wording throughout. Always begin with gratitude and turn your self-talk into productive proactive statements.

❖ _____

_____

❖ _____

_____

❖ _____

_____

- ❖ _____

- ❖ _____

AFFIRMATIONS

1. I am worthy of my dreams and goals.
2. I am motivated, beautiful, strong, deserving, blessed, empowered, prosperous, creating, intelligent, bold, growing, learning, living, inventing, unstoppable, inspired, and achieving.
3. I am devoted to my soul's purpose and passion.
4. I am confident, magnetic, and optimistic.
5. I believe in everything I do.
6. I am balanced and glowing.
7. I am always being guided to the path of my highest good.
8. I am expanding beyond what I believe is possible.
9. I am wealthy and prosperous in all aspects of my life.
10. I manifest everything I desire by believing and knowing it exists.

These affirmations can be a little different, but write ten of them. They can be the intentions you want to set, or you can focus on one intention and right ten affirmations to support that intention.

- ❖ _____
- ❖ _____
- ❖ _____
- ❖ _____
- ❖ _____

Practicing LOVE JOURNAL EDITION

- ❖ _____
- ❖ _____
- ❖ _____
- ❖ _____
- ❖ _____

LAW OF ABUNDANCE AND PROSPERITY

ABUNDANCE

Now to him who is able to do far more abundantly than all that we ask or think, according to the power at work within us.
—Ephesians 3:20

By creating visualizations of abundance in our lives, we draw this beautiful energy of success and dreams into our reality. You have within yourself everything required to make you thrive. Everything is abundant. The universe is abundant; you can never ask for too much. Money is abundant. Life is abundant. Beauty is abundant.

Never put yourself in competition with someone else. Everything is abundant. Always remember that there is enough for each and every one of us. I mean, put it in perspective: they make the same movies all the time. Two that come to mind are *No Strings Attached* and *Friends with Benefits*. Instead of feeling in competition, we can figure out a way to work together to make us all prosper.

PROSPERITY

The first step in achieving prosperity and wealth is learning to appreciate what you already have.
—Anonymous

We all draw from the universal energy pool according to our consciousness. The Spiritual Law of Prosperity dictates that if we believe we do not deserve prosperity, then we cannot rightly expect to receive it. If we expect prosperity, then we can expect to receive it.

We either have a "poverty consciousness" or an "abundance consciousness." Some people spend a great deal of their energy focusing on lack. Both conscious and subconscious fears underlie a poverty consciousness.

Greed and hoarding are like financial indigestion. If we hoard money in a bank account without allowing it to flow freely, eventually the message will reach the universe that we do not want or need more, and the supply will dry up. If we believe we are unworthy of receiving, then we will miss opportunities.

If we are tightfisted, mean-spirited, and/or rigid minded, we will never feel happy or content, as poverty consciousness is our belief and attitude. Those of us who are open-minded, generous, and giving will always be happy and content within. An attitude of prosperity leads us to use our riches with wisdom.

How to Incorporate Change?

❖ Determine how you feel about another's prosperity. Think about a time in your life when one of your friends or colleagues won a big promotion or a large sum of money. Answer this question honestly: Were you happy for them? If you secretly felt envy or jealousy for their success, you may want to address why you had those feelings. It is these feelings that are diminishing your own prosperity.

_____

_____

_____

_____

_____

_____

_____

❖ Determine how you feel about your own prosperity. Do you feel you have a right to prosperity? Do you feel you are worthy of the money that has come to you? It is these feelings that are diminishing your prosperity.

_____

_____

_____

_____

_____

_____

_____

❖ Cease all criticisms of other people's prosperity. Praise them and let them know you are proud of them.

❖ When you find yourself in a situation where you are complaining about all the lack in your life, stop and create an abundance list. Do you have your health? You have abundance. Do you have a roof over your head? You have abundance. Do you have food in the refrigerator? You guessed it—you have abundance.

❖ _____
❖ _____
❖ _____
❖ _____
❖ _____
❖ _____
❖ _____
❖ _____
❖ _____
❖ _____
❖ _____
❖ _____
❖ _____
❖ _____
❖ _____
❖ _____
❖ _____
❖ _____
❖ _____
❖ _____
❖ _____
❖ _____

❖ If you think you are experiencing shortages, think again. The universe may be trying to supply you with what you need, but you may be turning down the gifts. Ask yourself "Where in my life am I resisting? Where am I saying no? What would I do if I had no fear?"

❖ Is what you are thinking manufactured fear or true fear? Scarcity thinking is very much based on manufactured fear, which has its roots in the fear-based concept "I will not get my share." In addition, it is usually strengthened through worry about possible scenarios in an imaginary future situation filled with doom and gloom. True fear, on the other hand, is our body's warning mechanism. It is the fight-or-flight mechanism we use for our survival. Unfortunately, most people in society are operating on the manufactured fear model. Throughout your day, take the time to ask yourself "Is this situation real, or am I manufacturing fear?" If you are manufacturing fear, you are wasting precious energy.

FIVE THINGS

List five times you felt completely fulfilled and abundant.

- ❖ _____
- ❖ _____
- ❖ _____
- ❖ _____
- ❖ _____

List five times when you felt prosperous.

- ❖ _____
- ❖ _____
- ❖ _____
- ❖ _____
- ❖ _____

What were those feelings?

_____
_____
_____
_____
_____

What were you finally letting go of that made you feel abundant?

_____
_____
_____
_____
_____

What do you need to focus on to stay in an abundant mindset?

_____
_____
_____
_____
_____

AFFIRMATIONS

1. I prosper wherever I turn.
2. I *am* open to receive.
3. I *am* living a life of abundance and health.
4. There is plenty for everyone, and we bless and prosper each other.
5. My income is constantly increasing.
6. I live in the paradise of my own creation.
7. I act as if I already have what I want—it's an excellent way to attract happiness in my life.
8. I have the courage to live my dreams.
9. Fear no longer hinders my ability to live prosperously.
10. I am courageous.

It's that time in the chapter where you get to put your abundant mind to work and write down ten affirmations of abundance and prosperity.

- ❖ _____
- ❖ _____
- ❖ _____
- ❖ _____
- ❖ _____
- ❖ _____
- ❖ _____
- ❖ _____
- ❖ _____
- ❖ _____

PART 3:
THE LAWS OF HIGHER AWARENESS

LAW OF KARMA

How people treat you is their karma; how you react is yours.
—Wayne Dyer

Nothing happens by chance or outside the universal laws. There are no coincidences in life. I repeat: there are absolutely no coincidences in life! Every action (including your thoughts) has a reaction or consequence.

Every effect you see in your outside or physical world has a very specific cause that has its origin in your inner or mental world. Every one of your thoughts, words, or actions sets a specific effect in motion that will come to materialize over time. Know there is nothing such as chance or luck. Are you sensing a pattern here?

This law applies across all three planes: the spiritual, mental, and physical. Know that when you focus on your chosen goals with intention, that which you want to create in the physical world is automatically manifested in the spiritual world, and with perseverance, practice, and continued concentrated thought, it will start to materialize in the physical world.

How to Incorporate Change?

- ❖ The "Why?" exercise. This technique was initially developed by Sakichi Toyoda and used by Toyota to revolutionize its manufacturing approach. It explores the cause-and-effect relationships underlying a particular problem. By repeating the question "Why?" you dig deeper into the root cause. This exercise is a shorter version — you get to ask "Why?" three times only. You always have a good answer for the first "Why?" The second "Why?" becomes more difficult to answer. The third one makes you realize that, most probably, you don't know what you are doing. You can apply this when you are about to make a decision, when you are feeling confused and don't know what's going on, when you want to answer any question in your life, or when you need to come up with new ideas or solutions. By asking "Why?" three times, you get more clarity about who you are and why you are here.

❖ Problem: _____

  ❖ Why?
  _____
  _____
  _____

  ❖ Why?
  _____
  _____
  _____

  ❖ Why?
  _____
  _____
  _____

❖ Problem: _____

  ❖ Why?
  _____
  _____
  _____

  ❖ Why?
  _____
  _____
  _____

  ❖ Why?
  _____
  _____
  _____

- Problem: _____
  - Why?
    _____
    _____
    _____

  - Why?
    _____
    _____
    _____

  - Why?
    _____
    _____
    _____

- Write your own obituary.

_____
_____
_____
_____
_____
_____
_____
_____
_____
_____
_____

_____
_____
_____
_____
_____
_____
_____
_____
_____
_____
_____
_____
_____
_____
_____
_____

- ❖ Ask for feedback.
- ❖ Get an accountability partner.
- ❖ Don't argue with negative people. Don't get drawn in. Trust me, I know this gets hard, with political poison, divisiveness, and people trying to pit us against each other. Don't fall into that trap. If you look at the world as a loving place, love will surround you in every sense of the term.
- ❖ Of course, you always hear this, so I will just reiterate: surround yourself with positive people.
- ❖ Recognize when you are falling into negative thinking patterns. Some signs that you are falling into a negative thought pattern include limiting your thoughts to black-and-white beliefs without considering anything in the middle, trying to predict the future, making overgeneralizations, and catastrophizing small events.
- ❖ And possibly the best one: stop complaining! Yeah, another "duh!" But freaking do it, and stop making excuses. Those might be two steps, but I am lumping them into one because they're so similar they don't need separate bullet points.
- ❖ I have said this before, but it is worth reiterating: stop gossiping. It's hard because sometimes you love to sulk, but knock it off.

FIVE THINGS

List five things that you think have affected your karma. Have you ever cheated? Been involved in a hit-and-run accident? Lied? Tried to rip someone off? I think you get the point. Name five times when you were not such a great person, when someone would say "Oh, they are finally getting their karma."

❖ _____

❖ _____

❖ _____

❖ _____

❖ _____

Now you are going to list five things that will improve your karma. For example, let's say you committed a hit-and-run. You could buy gas for a stranger at the gas station, or if you don't have money, offer to wash your neighbor's car. That's just an example of a possible way to restore your karma. An admirable way is volunteering your time. If you cheated, you could volunteer with Big Brothers Big Sisters of America or kids' clubs. These are just examples, so think of creative ways to redeem your karma.

❖ _____

❖ _____
_____

❖ _____
_____

❖ _____
_____

❖ _____
_____

AFFIRMATIONS

1. I devote a portion of my time to helping others. It is good for my own health.
2. I only speak positively about those in my world. Negativity has no part in my life.
3. The more peaceful I am inside, the more peace I have to share with others.
4. I am respected as I respect others.
5. What I give out returns to me.
6. I am grateful that I naturally attract positive karma and positive vibes.
7. I am grateful that I have paid off all my karmic debts, now and in the future.
8. I accept my losses and give thanks to the universe for the lessons I have learned.
9. My karma is always improving.
10. I am happily rooted in the present and gratefully allow the purifying power of my consciousness to clean the slate of my past.

Write down affirmations that will help heal your karma. Yes, it is still ten of them. Always ten, no less. You can write more if you want to. I will let you.

- ❖ _____
- ❖ _____
- ❖ _____
- ❖ _____
- ❖ _____
- ❖ _____
- ❖ _____
- ❖ _____
- ❖ _____
- ❖ _____

LAW OF RESPONSIBILITY

The price of greatness is responsibility.
—Winston Churchill

You are solely responsible for everything you are, for everything you have (or don't have), for everything you achieve, and for everything you become. As such, there is no room for excuses or complaints, and there is certainly never anyone or anything to blame for your life—not the government, not society, not other people. You have attracted these events and circumstances via your thoughts through the Law of Attraction and the resulting choices you have made. As such, you are entirely responsible for *everything* and therefore also hold the power to change *anything* by choosing a different set of thoughts that will lead you toward making a different set of choices.

Given this, you must always accept the full consequences of the choices you have made. After all, these choices have shaped your life up to this point, and now, in this moment, you have the choice yet again to shape it any which way you choose. Only through complete responsibility will you make the progress you desire to make in life. When you play victim and don't accept responsibility, you will bring in more of the same challenges and people.

With this law, you are cognizant of no longer playing the victim card. No one is out to get you, and if they are, you are drawing them to you. There are a lot of things in life I blame other people for. This is where I get to shed them. I get to shed my abandonment issues and my trust issues to become a confident and worthy woman deserving of love.

We all have these stories in our heads. The "I will never be good enough" mentality gets to stop now. "This person did this, so I did this" gets to stop now. Our mistakes are our lessons to learn from.

How to Incorporate Change?

❖ "I did that." As you move throughout your day, consciously acknowledge everything that happens to you. Take responsibility for all the good, bad, and ugly by telling yourself "I did that." For example, if you are running late and everything seems to be going wrong, stop and say "I did that." Don't chastise yourself. Stop and acknowledge your responsibility. Then shift to a new state of being.

- ❖ Create a vision board. It makes you think about what you really want. It helps you get unstuck. It's a nice daily reminder of your aspirations. Plus, it's fun to visualize.
- ❖ Stop assuming what other people are thinking.
- ❖ Don't dwell on the past.
- ❖ Live your life not for others but for yourself.
- ❖ The biggest, most important one is to stop blaming others for ALL of your problems.

Five Things

List five things you take responsibility for, things you have blamed on others in the past. The hardest part for most people to accept is responsibility. They like to deflect when they did something wrong and don't want to admit it. When you never take responsibility, people begin to notice it, and they see you in a not-so-fond light. People would much rather have someone take responsibility for their mistakes than always blame someone else or something that made them screw up.

- ❖ _____
- ❖ _____
- ❖ _____
- ❖ _____
- ❖ _____

AFFIRMATIONS

1. It is safe to look within.
2. I am deeply fulfilled by all that I do.
3. I honor who I am.
4. I drink lots of water to cleanse my body and mind.
5. I transform negative energy into love and light.
6. Loving others is easy when I love and accept myself.
7. I live in limitless love, light, and joy.
8. I enjoy the foods that are best for my body.
9. I balance my life between work, rest, and play.
10. I accept responsibility for all of my choices.

Write your best affirmations yet. Free yourself from victimhood. Take responsibility. We all know we like to blame others because we don't want to be wrong or show our faults, but it is through humility that we gain strength, perseverance, and trust.

❖ _____

❖ _____

❖ _____

❖ _____

❖ _____

❖ _____

❖ _____

❖ _____

❖ _____

❖ _____

LAW OF FORGIVENESS

Forgiveness does not change the past, but it does enlarge the future.
—Paul Boese

Forgiveness is the ultimate gift to we can offer to ourselves and others. It opens a channel of healing and grace that transcends the boundaries we place around ourselves. It is tolerant and loving and brings a peaceful balance to the soul. It allows the co-creative energy of love to inspire and lead us to a life of fulfillment. There is no greater sacrifice than bringing forth forgiveness to those who we perceive have brought injustice into our lives. Whether we are forgiving a simple act of unkindness or an act that altered our lives significantly, there can be no energetic healing without forgiveness.

When we hold on to resentment and anger, we shut down our hearts. We live in a reality where control dominates our lives instead of letting the natural flow of energy move through us. There is no legitimate satisfaction in harboring negative emotions, only the misperception that we are holding others accountable for their actions. In truth, we are all held accountable for our thoughts and actions within the "Divine Matrix" of energetic principles. (Between 1993 and 2000, a series of groundbreaking experiments revealed dramatic evidence of a web of energy that connects everything in our lives and our world—the "Divine Matrix." This is also the title of a book by Greg Braden.)

Forgiveness frees the heart and mind; it's a necessary process for personal reconciliation. We hold on to our hate and anger like a badge of honor, refusing to see the larger picture within our spirituality. All experiences are within an illusion of perception, a dreamlike state we can shift and shape when our hearts are open. Forgiveness is a powerful force for energetic change that promotes personal and spiritual growth. If our goal is to create a more harmonious life, then forgiveness must be part of that process.

The same holds true for forgiveness of ourselves and the forgiveness that comes to us from others. Any act can be forgiven if we are willing to understand the truth this healing will bring to us. When two people join energies through the process of forgiveness, it changes their perspective. That energy has the ability to transform and inspire miracles.

All good comes from forgiveness. It is the truth that the continuation of life is due to man's being forgiving. By forgiving, the universe is held together.

As long as we harbor negative thoughts of anger, judgement, hatred, and intolerance for others, we cannot be happy, simply because while we harbor those feelings, we experience the results of them.

That's not how the mind works, unfortunately. The mind is always responding to feelings: that anger is anger and hatred is hatred, and while you are producing it, you are feeling it. Feelings create chemical reactions, and then negative hormones flood through your body, bathing every cell in chemicals that will make you sick and get old more quickly. There was a great experiment conducted by Dr. Masaru Emoto, who claimed water was a "blueprint for our reality" and that emotional energies and vibrations could change the physical structure of water. Emoto's water crystal experiments consisted of exposing water in glasses to different words, pictures, or music and then freezing and examining the aesthetic properties of the resulting crystals with microscopic photography. Emoto stated water exposed to positive speech and thoughts resulted in the formation of visually "pleasing" crystals when it was frozen, and negative intentions yielded "ugly" frozen crystal formations.

Forgiveness is not about the other person. Forgiveness is for you, to heal you. You may feel justified in holding on to punishing others, or you might feel you have every right to hold on to anger, but you must ask "Who am I hurting when I hold on to this anger and unforgiveness?" The person may not care or think about it as much as you do. Quit giving them that power over you. You know the answer is you. That person or those people may have hurt you in the past, but holding on to the unforgiveness means you carry on hurting yourself every time you relive the event and feel the feelings. Forgive, and you will be forgiven!

The word "forgive" has two syllables: "for" and "give." When you forgive, it simply means you "give" up being angry and intolerant "for" peace and harmony. You "give" up judgement and hatred "for" something else, perhaps acceptance and love.

If you find it difficult to forgive or you feel fully justified or entitled to be aggrieved, ask yourself "Would I rather be right or happy?" If you'd rather be right, carry on doing what you're doing and hold on to the merciless thoughts, but if you'd rather be happy, you'll have to let them go. Forgiving clears karmic debt. When you truly forgive others, you'll feel free.

You, too, can be forgiven when you feel true and genuine remorse for your transgressions. When you know in your heart that you have changed and you can truly say the new you will always be faithful, honest, and kind, you are forgiven.

How do you forgive yourself? Is it making amends to the people you hurt in the past? Do you need people to forgive you for what you have done to them, or can you forgive yourself no matter what the circumstances?

How to Incorporate change?

- ❖ Say "Thank you."
- ❖ Make a conscious effort to not talk disparagingly about others who have hurt you.
- ❖ It is important to figure out who hurt you and why. It is important to recognize the pain you are suffering from and acknowledge it. Lack of trust? Abuse? Self-loathing? Focus on forgiveness. If it is years later, try to make amends. This is easier said than done. I did it with my father, who wasn't present in my younger years. He regrets it, but we both forgave our pasts and now having an amazing relationship.
- ❖ Practice empathy. If you examine the details about the life of the person who harmed you, you can often see more clearly what wounds they carry and start to develop empathy for them. Imagine their life and what they have gone through. I know sometimes that is not an excuse, but you need to heal. If you continue to carry this burden of someone who possibly raped you and don't forgive, you will hurt your future relationships.
- ❖ Find meaning in your suffering and grow from it. How has this suffering made you a better person? What lesson did you take away?
- ❖ Last, but certainly not least, forgive yourself.
- ❖ See forgiveness as a gift to yourself and not as a gift to others.
- ❖ Stop ruminating over negative thoughts.
- ❖ Consider the impact of what holding a grudge does to you.

Five Things

List five people you want forgiveness from. Who have you hurt in the past who you would like to forgive you? This will be difficult and then refreshing. If they can't forgive you during this time, that is okay. That is on them. After that, let it go. That is not the type of negative situation you need in your life. In that moment, you can allow yourself to forgive you. Know in that moment, it is okay to forgive yourself, even if the other person is not ready.

- ❖ _____
- ❖ _____

- ❖ _____
- ❖ _____
- ❖ _____

List five people you need to forgive. It is time to let go of the negative past. It has helped you grow into the person you are today, either positive or negative, and it is now time to cut the negative cords and embrace what the future can bring. I know how hard it can be to forgive people, especially when some can't be helped because they have substance abuse problems or feel abandoned. It is extremely hard, but don't let those chains from the past hold you down. Don't let trust issues keep you from the love you deserve. Forgive and move on. Yes, it is easier to write than to do. It doesn't have to be done in a single afternoon. There is no time scale. Do it at the pace that's right for you when you are ready.

- ❖ _____
- ❖ _____
- ❖ _____
- ❖ _____
- ❖ _____

BONUS EXERCISE: ACKNOWLEDGMENT

This might be one of the hardest exercises in this entire book. This is where you have to dig deep within yourself. Pick five people who have hurt you the most, people who have hurt you in ways that you never thought imaginable. Five people who made you lose hope. Five people you don't know why were brought into your life to each you a lesson. Now you get to acknowledge them in a way that comes from love and compassion. Acknowledge the great accomplishments and the pressures they have endured with dignity and grace—how they have helped mold you into the person you are today. Remember, this is all about love and not about how they hurt you but how you learned to overcome these situations.

Dear _____,

_____

_____

_____

_____

_____

_____

_____

_____

_____

_____

_____

_____

_____

_____

_____

_____

_____

I forgive you,

_____

Practicing LOVE JOURNAL EDITION

Dear _____,

_____

_____

_____

_____

_____

_____

_____

_____

_____

_____

_____

_____

_____

_____

_____

I forgive you,

_____

Dear _____,

_____

_____

_____

_____

_____

_____

_____

_____

_____

_____

_____

_____

_____

_____

_____

_____

_____

I forgive you,

_____

Practicing LOVE JOURNAL EDITION

Dear _____,

_____

_____

_____

_____

_____

_____

_____

_____

_____

_____

_____

_____

_____

_____

_____

_____

I forgive you,

_____

Deb Bailey & Sarah Melland

Dear _____,

_____
_____
_____
_____
_____
_____
_____
_____
_____
_____
_____
_____
_____
_____
_____
_____
_____
_____
_____

I forgive you,

_____

AFFIRMATIONS

1. I forgive myself and set myself free.
2. As I forgive myself, it becomes easier to forgive others.
3. The past is over.
4. I forgive myself and release my worries to the Creator.
5. It is safe for me to release all of my childhood traumas and move into love.
6. I forgive everyone in my past for all perceived wrongs. I release them with love.
7. I acknowledge my faults and forgive myself completely.
8. Forgiveness is a gift to myself.
9. The past is done. I now live in the present.
10. I am forgiving, loving, gentle, and kind to everyone.

Write affirmations that state how you are forgiving the past that is holding you back. Write at least ten of them. At this point, affirmations should be flowing out of you. You can't stop. Just keep going. Free all your burdens and forgive. You finally get to be free.

- ❖ _____
- ❖ _____
- ❖ _____
- ❖ _____
- ❖ _____
- ❖ _____
- ❖ _____
- ❖ _____
- ❖ _____
- ❖ _____

PART 4:
THE LAWS OF HIGHER FREQUENCY

LAW OF NO JUDGEMENT

Do unto others as you would have them do to you.
—Matthew 7:12

The universal spirit does not judge us; judgements are human inventions—a way to compare, contrast, and control as we judge ourselves against artificial and often idealistic standards of false perfection. Under this law, our judgements attract judgement to us in equal measure.

We do not know judgement: we grow up learning judgement. We must break this vicious cycle. Do not teach your children how to judge, as they will become their own harshest critics.

We judge others because we have been conditioned to do so. We judge others according to what we hate in ourselves. Our own pain is more powerful that the pain of other people. Our own experience is more valuable than the experience of other people. Our own perspective is dearer to us than the perspective of other people. When we see others from our own perspective, we find other people wrong. From their perspective, we may be equally wrong.

One of the greatest books I have ever read is *Journey of Souls* by Dr. Michael Newton. If you haven't read it, I suggest doing so, as it will change your life. Newton, an atheist hypnotherapist, decided to hypnotize people to see what happens in the afterlife. After hypnotizing thousands of people, he began to draw some general conclusions, as their stories were eerily similar.

Without going into too much detail, as I suggest you read the whole book yourself, there was one particular story that stood out for me. We always seem to judge people by the way they dress or look if they are somewhere out of the norm, or at least what we think is normal. In this story, we all choose who we want to be before coming to this world. We choose all the lessons we want to learn in this life; we choose the people in our lives and how they will help bring us closer to God, the divine, the universe—whatever you choose to call it.

The particular story that melted my heart said we try to make our lives as difficult as we think we can withstand. We want to push ourselves closer to divine oneness and closer to enlightenment, compassion, and love. When we see someone walking down the street and we judge them, they chose that. When we see someone who is disabled, they chose that. They chose that difficult life because it's one of the toughest lives to navigate through in this world, so they learn more lessons than the people with easier lives.

Remember, we chose this life. We chose what country we wanted to live in, our ethnicity, our sexual orientation, and everything in between. Before you judge someone for being different, know they chose that life, and you chose yours. If someone has it easy and everything has been handed to them, they chose that life. They were not ready to endure the hardships you are going through. You chose your hardships, and they were never meant to defeat you. You chose them because you knew you could conquer them. Before you pass judgement, remember that.

How to Incorporate Change?

- ❖ **Don't pass judgment.** If you find yourself being judgmental, stop yourself. This takes a greater awareness than we usually have, so the first step (and an important one) is to observe your thoughts for a few days, trying to notice when you're being judgmental. This can be a difficult step. Remind yourself to observe. Once you're more aware, you can then stop yourself when you feel yourself being judgmental, even (or especially) if putting someone down gives you a good laugh.
- ❖ **Understand.** Instead of judging someone for what they've done or how they look, try instead to understand the person. Put yourself in their shoes. Try to imagine their background. If possible, talk to them. Find out their backstory. Everyone has one. If you can't find out their story, try to imagine the circumstances that might have led the person to act or look like they do.
- ❖ **Accept.** Once you begin to understand, or at least think you kind of understand, try to accept. Accept that person for who they are without trying to change them. Accept they will act the way they do without wanting them to change. The world is what it is, and as much as you try, you can only change a little bit of it. It will continue to be as it is long after you're gone. Accept that, because otherwise, you're in for a world of frustration.
- ❖ **Love.** Once you've accepted someone for who they are, try to love them, even if you don't know them. Even if you've hated them in the past. No matter who they are, old or young, light skinned or dark, male or female, rich or poor. Love them.
- ❖ **Practice empathy.** It will help you build social connections with others and regulate your own emotions.
- ❖ **Give compliments.** If you feel the need to judge someone and it slips out, the next step is to give that person one compliment. Yes, it has to be a genuine compliment, and yes, you have to mean it.
- ❖ **Stop name-calling.** Even under your breath. Even in your car at a driver who just cut you off. Even when they can't hear you.

Five Things

Make a list of five things you tend to judge the most in people.

- ❖ _____
- ❖ _____
- ❖ _____
- ❖ _____
- ❖ _____

Why do you do that, and how are you going to change so you stop judging?

_____
_____
_____
_____
_____

How are you going to come from a place of compassion and gratitude?

_____
_____
_____
_____

What needs to happen for you to make this change?

___

Why do you feel the need to be judgmental? What triggers it?

___

What is missing in your life that makes you feel the need to judge?

___

How can you stop the negative back talk?

_____

_____

_____

_____

_____

AFFIRMATIONS

1. I am loved, and I am at peace.
2. I get to guide the direction of my thinking; eventually, the most nurtured thoughts become my truths.
3. I have compassion for all.
4. I love my family members just as they are. I do not try to change anyone.
5. Everyone is worthy of love and empathy.
6. I am willing to release judgment because I am ready to be free.
7. I foster peace in myself so I can bring people into my peace.
8. I increase my energy by choosing to love rather than judge. I expand my energy by giving love, receiving love, and promoting love.
9. I treat people in pain with compassion, not more pain.
10. I send love to the people who need it most and clear the blocks that keep us apart.

It's your favorite part of the book—affirmation time! Let's do this! Write ten affirmations about compassion, empathy, and, most importantly, love. You are no longer a judgmental person; you are a beautiful, loving being who sees everyone equally.

❖ _____

❖ _____

Practicing LOVE JOURNAL EDITION

- ❖ _____
- ❖ _____
- ❖ _____
- ❖ _____
- ❖ _____
- ❖ _____
- ❖ _____
- ❖ _____

LAW OF UNCONDITIONAL LOVE AND GRATITUDE

If you go out of your way to express unconditional love, you automatically rise above fear.
—Anonymous

Miracles are an expression of unconditional love. The Christ Consciousness is a message of love and service to others shared by all major religions. Loving without judgement or reservation increases the awareness that we are all part of a divine energy we call God. We create miracles every day when we express our divine love and gratitude for one another. It is simple yet so difficult to integrate into our lives when we feel victimized by others and the world we live in. When we love without condition or restraint, we connect in a profound manner with the divine energy. The beauty in life becomes more apparent, and we find ourselves immersed in the light of creation. Love flows through us and reminds us that we are all unique and valuable. We are each an incredible expression of love. Love of self is the foundation for accepting ourselves and others despite our imperfections.

Unconditional love is not selfish or demanding but accepting of others without judgement or expectation. It transcends our own desires and focuses on the needs of others. It is the basis for our belief in service to others as a spiritual community. When we bring love into our lives more fully, we raise our vibrations and the vibration of others energetically. We become catalysts for positive change. Love is the energetic connection for all things. It transforms all we think and feel about ourselves and our world. It rises above self-pity and makes us grateful for what is good in our lives.

Gratitude, like unconditional love, resonates within the heart's energy. That energy creates our reality when it's joined with corresponding thoughts. Positive emotions and thoughts create positive outcomes, and the same is true for negative emotions and thoughts. Love and gratitude are the energies of balance and harmony. When a person practices love in their life, gratitude is generally present, opening them up to receiving divine inspiration and abundance.

How to Incorporate Change?

- ❖ Think of someone who frustrates you. Identify three positive attributes about that person. Now think of three reasons why that person is worthy of love. After you are finished, still your mind and visualize love flowing from your heart to that particular person. After doing this, you will see immediate signs of improvement in your relationship.

- ❖ Who Frustrates you? _____
  - ❖ Positive Attribute? _____
  - ❖ Positive Attribute? _____
  - ❖ Positive Attribute? _____
- ❖ Who Frustrates you? _____
  - ❖ Positive Attribute? _____
  - ❖ Positive Attribute? _____
  - ❖ Positive Attribute? _____
- ❖ Who Frustrates you? _____
  - ❖ Positive Attribute? _____
  - ❖ Positive Attribute? _____
  - ❖ Positive Attribute? _____
- ❖ Who Frustrates you? _____
  - ❖ Positive Attribute? _____
  - ❖ Positive Attribute? _____
  - ❖ Positive Attribute? _____
- ❖ Who Frustrates you? _____
  - ❖ Positive Attribute? _____
  - ❖ Positive Attribute? _____
  - ❖ Positive Attribute? _____

- ❖ Do something to demonstrate you love yourself. Eat healthy (I recommend alkaline). Buy yourself flowers. Take a long, leisurely bath. Take a day off. Call into work and tell them "I am too well to come in today." Spend the day doing something you enjoy.
- ❖ Go on a negativity diet. Stop berating yourself. Stop berating other people. Stop complaining about the weather.
- ❖ Practice loving acts of outrageous kindness.
- ❖ Stop reading the newspapers and watching the news. Read only inspirational materials.

Five Things

Make a gratitude list. This is a list you will look back on frequently and every day when you are feeling out of sorts or down. Make this list as complete as possible, from your clean underwear, to running water, to the most utterly ridiculous thing you are grateful for. Anything and everything goes. Embrace the beautiful life you lead. Even the simplest things make us grateful.

- ❖ _____
- ❖ _____
- ❖ _____
- ❖ _____
- ❖ _____
- ❖ _____
- ❖ _____
- ❖ _____
- ❖ _____
- ❖ _____
- ❖ _____
- ❖ _____
- ❖ _____
- ❖ _____
- ❖ _____
- ❖ _____

Practicing LOVE JOURNAL EDITION

❖ _____
❖ _____
❖ _____
❖ _____
❖ _____
❖ _____
❖ _____
❖ _____
❖ _____
❖ _____
❖ _____
❖ _____
❖ _____
❖ _____

Affirmations

1. I am comfortable looking in the mirror and saying "I love you. I really love you."
2. Deep at the center of my being is an infinite well of love.
3. My day begins and ends with gratitude.
4. Loving others is easy when I love and accept myself.

5. I choose to see clearly with the eyes of love.
6. I am worthy.
7. I am enough.
8. I love myself unconditionally, and I am grateful every day for who I am.
9. I speak to myself in loving ways because I deeply respect and appreciate myself.
10. I choose to see the love in everything and everyone.

These ten affirmations should be the easiest affirmations you have to write. You get to show your gratitude. You get to show how amazed you are at how beautiful life is in this moment and how thankful you are for this beautiful experience.

❖ _____

❖ _____

❖ _____

❖ _____

❖ _____

❖ _____

❖ _____

❖ _____

❖ _____

❖ _____

LAW OF ONENESS

Each person you meet is an aspect of yourself, clamoring for love.
—Eric Micha'el Leventhal

We are all part of a great energy. This great energy can be called source, God, the universe, or whatever you deem necessary. In this book, we call it love. The law simply states that we all come from one source, and since we all come from that one source, we are that source, and we all are one. All are creations of the All and have our soul existence solely within the infinite mind of the All. We all interact with each other on a subconscious level as well.

We operate as one energy source. We can increase and decrease our vibration when we are love-minded people. Our energy, our vibration, is intensified, bringing us closer to the source and the higher frequency of ascension. If we act out of hate, our energy and vibration are very low and keep us more grounded and blocked. Because we are all one, everything you think, say, or do affects every other soul.

How to Incorporate Change?

- ❖ See everything and everyone as source energy in action. As you go about your day, mentally visualize everyone and everything as the source energy spark. We are all one.
- ❖ See everything and everyone as yourself in action, as told in the beautiful short story "The Egg." They are you, and you are them.
- ❖ Go outside and spend at least thirty minutes connecting to the ground. Feel the fresh grass between your toes. Listen to the sounds of nature—the leaves rustling, the birds chirping, even how the sunlight hits all the objects surrounding you perfectly. Even if it's not sunny, look at all the abundance nature has to offer.
- ❖ Always be mindful of your words and actions because they directly affect those connected with them. If you cut someone off in traffic, then you have precipitated negative sentiment in that person. If you say something condescending to someone else, those words can have

a profound effect on that person in terms of their self-esteem and what they think of themselves.

- ❖ Go out of your normal routine and try to compliment everyone you come in contact with today. Make them genuine compliments. You can do it on social media. Do whatever you can today to start a ripple effect of positive change in the world.

FIVE THINGS

List five things you want to do to improve a stranger's day. It could be as simple as paying for their coffee in line at Starbucks or giving a compliment—you name it. The world is your oyster. Be creative, and most of all, always have fun with it. I know this might take some of you out of your comfort zone, and your ego is going insane, asking hundreds of questions: "What if they don't want to be complimented?" "What if they aren't grateful in return?" and all the other stories you are telling yourself. Stop for one moment. It is okay. You can do things for strangers that they don't notice, such as cleaning up litter or volunteering at shelters. Sit on it for a bit and think of the best way you know how to make someone's day. It doesn't have to be about money, and I prefer that it isn't, but if this is the way you choose to improve a stranger's day, it should cost less than $20.

- ❖ _____
- ❖ _____
- ❖ _____
- ❖ _____
- ❖ _____

List five ways you are going to improve your friend's or family member's day. Maybe surprise them with flowers at work. Call them just to say hi if you haven't caught up in a while. Again, be creative, and get out of your comfort zone as much as possible.

- ❖

- ❖ _____
- ❖ _____
- ❖ _____
- ❖ _____

AFFIRMATIONS

1. I am divinely guided and protected at all times.
2. We are all family, and the planet is our home.
3. I am safe in the universe, and all life loves and supports me.
4. I trust the universe to help me see the good in everything and everyone.
5. We are all eternal spirit.
6. I am aligned with my highest good, allowing good for all.
7. In our hearts, we are all one.
8. I feel harmony between myself and the universe around me.
9. I am thankful for each and every person I come into contact with, knowing we are all here at the same time for the greater good.
10. I am in touch with the universe, and I use it for the good of the community.

Now, these are your last affirmations! Make them count!

- ❖ _____
- ❖ _____
- ❖ _____
- ❖ _____
- ❖ _____

- ❖ _____
- ❖ _____
- ❖ _____
- ❖ _____
- ❖ _____

CLOSING WORDS

It is good to have an end to journey toward; but it is the journey that matters, in the end.
—Ernest Hemingway

Everything is energy. All thought and emotion vibrate with a resonance that creates the world we see. If we understand the principles of that energy, we can use the information to effect change in our lives and the world. Thoughts and emotions drive our behavior. Self-reflection—both consciously and through mindful meditation—about what we think and feel and the way we direct those thoughts and emotions is the key to moving out of the box we call our belief system and into new ways of living a more abundant and fulfilling life. It is when we allow ourselves to become vulnerable to the truth of how we are living our lives that we can free ourselves from old patterns. If we can identify the beliefs that aren't serving us in a positive way, we can focus on creating a better outcome. With practice, it is possible to change our perceptions of challenging situations and how we react to them. Change takes patience and determination, but the rewards are life altering.

Every experience helps us understand our own specific needs and brings us closer to our authentic selves. When we look at our lives, it is more important to identify what we want to change than to feel limited by a sense of failure or regret. Free will gives us the power to decide what we want to do with our lives—whether we remain feeling like victims of our personal experiences or take responsibility for how we contribute to our current life circumstances. Ask yourself "Am I happy, and do I have joy in my life?" If not, are you ready to make the conscious decision to initiate changes in your life?

To make sense of our lives is to embrace the knowledge that we are all on personal and collective journeys of spiritual enlightenment—journeys leading us to learn to love ourselves and one another unconditionally. We are more than the external world communicates to us. We are thoughtful spiritual beings living a physical experience designed to further our understanding of our connectedness to God and one another. We are on a path to transcending our physical limitations. We are mind, body, and spirit vibrating together through the miracle of creation. We resonate with the vibration of love when we allow it to enter our lives. That energy is the pulse of God, the Divine Consciousness.

Meditation Journal

MEDITATION SESSION #1

Believe you can and you're halfway there.
—Theodore Roosevelt

Length of Session:

Time of Day:

Reflect on the following experiences and describe in detail.

What is your intention?

_____
_____

Visual Experience (what were you seeing)

_____
_____
_____
_____
_____

Emotional Experience (what were you feeling)

_____
_____
_____
_____
_____

Mental Experience (what were you thinking)

_____

_____

_____

_____

_____

Physical Experience (what were you sensing)

_____

_____

_____

_____

_____

Final Impressions

_____

_____

_____

_____

_____

_____

_____

_____

_____

_____

MEDITATION SESSION #2

Try to be a rainbow in someone's cloud.
—Maya Angelou

Length of Session:

Time of Day:

Reflect on the following experiences and describe in detail.

What is your intention?
_____
_____

Visual Experience (what were you seeing)
_____
_____
_____
_____
_____

Emotional Experience (what were you feeling)
_____
_____
_____
_____
_____

Mental Experience (what were you thinking)

_____
_____
_____
_____
_____

Physical Experience (what were you sensing)

_____
_____
_____
_____
_____

Final Impressions

_____
_____
_____
_____
_____
_____
_____
_____
_____
_____
_____

MEDITATION SESSION #3

Nothing is impossible, the word itself says 'I'm possible'!
—Audrey Hepburn

Length of Session:

Time of Day:

Reflect on the following experiences and describe in detail.

What is your intention?

_____
_____

Visual Experience (what were you seeing)

_____
_____
_____
_____
_____

Emotional Experience (what were you feeling)

_____
_____
_____
_____
_____

Mental Experience (what were you thinking)

Physical Experience (what were you sensing)

Final Impressions

MEDITATION SESSION #4

In a gentle way, you can shake the world.
—Mahatma Gandhi

Length of Session:

Time of Day:

Reflect on the following experiences and describe in detail.

What is your intention?

_____
_____

Visual Experience (what were you seeing)

_____
_____
_____
_____
_____

Emotional Experience (what were you feeling)

_____
_____
_____
_____
_____

Mental Experience (what were you thinking)

___

Physical Experience (what were you sensing)

___

Final Impressions

___

MEDITATION SESSION #5

Clouds come floating into my life, no longer to carry rain or usher storm, but to add color to my sunset sky.
—Rabindranath Tagore

Length of Session:

Time of Day:

Reflect on the following experiences and describe in detail.

What is your intention?

_____
_____

Visual Experience (what were you seeing)

_____
_____
_____
_____
_____

Emotional Experience (what were you feeling)

_____
_____
_____
_____
_____

Mental Experience (what were you thinking)

_____
_____
_____
_____
_____

Physical Experience (what were you sensing)

_____
_____
_____
_____
_____

Final Impressions

_____
_____
_____
_____
_____
_____
_____
_____
_____
_____
_____

MEDITATION SESSION #6

Each day provides its own gifts.
—Marcus Aurelius

Length of Session:

Time of Day:

Reflect on the following experiences and describe in detail.

What is your intention?
_____
_____

Visual Experience (what were you seeing)
_____
_____
_____
_____
_____

Emotional Experience (what were you feeling)
_____
_____
_____
_____
_____

Mental Experience (what were you thinking)

_____

_____

_____

_____

_____

Physical Experience (what were you sensing)

_____

_____

_____

_____

_____

Final Impressions

_____

_____

_____

_____

_____

_____

_____

_____

_____

_____

_____

_____

_____

MEDITATION SESSION #7

What we think, we become
—Buddha

Length of Session:

Time of Day:

Reflect on the following experiences and describe in detail.

What is your intention?
_____
_____

Visual Experience (what were you seeing)
_____
_____
_____
_____
_____

Emotional Experience (what were you feeling)
_____
_____
_____
_____
_____

Mental Experience (what were you thinking)

Physical Experience (what were you sensing)

Final Impressions

MEDITATION SESSION #8

If we did all the things we are capable of, we would literally astound ourselves.
—Thomas A. Edison

Length of Session:

Time of Day:

Reflect on the following experiences and describe in detail.

What is your intention?
_____
_____

Visual Experience (what were you seeing)
_____
_____
_____
_____
_____

Emotional Experience (what were you feeling)
_____
_____
_____
_____
_____

Mental Experience (what were you thinking)

_____
_____
_____
_____
_____

Physical Experience (what were you sensing)

_____
_____
_____
_____
_____

Final Impressions

_____
_____
_____
_____
_____
_____
_____
_____
_____
_____
_____
_____

MEDITATION SESSION #9

Whoever is happy will make others happy too.
—Anne Frank

Length of Session:

Time of Day:

Reflect on the following experiences and describe in detail.

What is your intention?

_____
_____

Visual Experience (what were you seeing)

_____
_____
_____
_____
_____

Emotional Experience (what were you feeling)

_____
_____
_____
_____
_____

Mental Experience (what were you thinking)

_____
_____
_____
_____
_____

Physical Experience (what were you sensing)

_____
_____
_____
_____
_____

Final Impressions

_____
_____
_____
_____
_____
_____
_____
_____
_____
_____
_____

MEDITATION SESSION #10

Beliefs creates the actual fact.
—William James

Length of Session:

Time of Day:

Reflect on the following experiences and describe in detail.

What is your intention?
_____
_____

Visual Experience (what were you seeing)
_____
_____
_____
_____
_____

Emotional Experience (what were you feeling)
_____
_____
_____
_____
_____

Mental Experience (what were you thinking)

_____
_____
_____
_____
_____

Physical Experience (what were you sensing)

_____
_____
_____
_____
_____

Final Impressions

_____
_____
_____
_____
_____
_____
_____
_____
_____
_____
_____
_____

MEDITATION SESSION #11

Change your thoughts and you change your world.
—Norman Vincent Peale

Length of Session:

Time of Day:

Reflect on the following experiences and describe in detail.

What is your intention?

_____
_____

Visual Experience (what were you seeing)

_____
_____
_____
_____
_____

Emotional Experience (what were you feeling)

_____
_____
_____
_____
_____

Mental Experience (what were you thinking)

___

Physical Experience (what were you sensing)

___

Final Impressions

___

MEDITATION SESSION #12

What great thing would you attempt if you knew you could not fail?
—Robert H. Schuller

Length of Session:

Time of Day:

Reflect on the following experiences and describe in detail.

What is your intention?

_____

_____

Visual Experience (what were you seeing)

_____

_____

_____

_____

_____

Emotional Experience (what were you feeling)

_____

_____

_____

_____

_____

Mental Experience (what were you thinking)

_____
_____
_____
_____
_____

Physical Experience (what were you sensing)

_____
_____
_____
_____
_____

Final Impressions

_____
_____
_____
_____
_____
_____
_____
_____
_____
_____
_____

MEDITATION SESSION #13

You are always free to change your mind and choose a different future, or a different past.
—Richard Bach

Length of Session:

Time of Day:

Reflect on the following experiences and describe in detail.

What is your intention?

_____
_____

Visual Experience (what were you seeing)

_____
_____
_____
_____
_____

Emotional Experience (what were you feeling)

_____
_____
_____
_____
_____

Mental Experience (what were you thinking)

_____
_____
_____
_____
_____

Physical Experience (what were you sensing)

_____
_____
_____
_____
_____

Final Impressions

_____
_____
_____
_____
_____
_____
_____
_____
_____
_____
_____

MEDITATION SESSION #14

Out of difficulties grow miracles.
—Jean de la Bruyere

Length of Session:

Time of Day:

Reflect on the following experiences and describe in detail.

What is your intention?
_____
_____

Visual Experience (what were you seeing)
_____
_____
_____
_____
_____

Emotional Experience (what were you feeling)
_____
_____
_____
_____
_____

Mental Experience (what were you thinking)

_____
_____
_____
_____
_____

Physical Experience (what were you sensing)

_____
_____
_____
_____
_____

Final Impressions

_____
_____
_____
_____
_____
_____
_____
_____
_____
_____
_____

MEDITATION SESSION #15

Enjoy the little things, for one day you may look back and realize they were big things.
—Robert Brault

Length of Session:

Time of Day:

Reflect on the following experiences and describe in detail.

What is your intention?

_____
_____

Visual Experience (what were you seeing)

_____
_____
_____
_____
_____

Emotional Experience (what were you feeling)

_____
_____
_____
_____
_____

Mental Experience (what were you thinking)

_____
_____
_____
_____
_____

Physical Experience (what were you sensing)

_____
_____
_____
_____
_____

Final Impressions

_____
_____
_____
_____
_____
_____
_____
_____
_____
_____

MEDITATION SESSION #16

It's a funny thing about life, once you begin to take note of the things you are grateful for, you begin to lose sight of the things you lack.
—Germany Kent

Length of Session:

Time of Day:

Reflect on the following experiences and describe in detail.

What is your intention?

_____
_____

Visual Experience (what were you seeing)

_____
_____
_____
_____
_____

Emotional Experience (what were you feeling)

_____
_____
_____
_____
_____

Mental Experience (what were you thinking)

_____
_____
_____
_____
_____

Physical Experience (what were you sensing)

_____
_____
_____
_____
_____

Final Impressions

_____
_____
_____
_____
_____
_____
_____
_____
_____
_____
_____

MEDITATION SESSION #17

If the only prayer you said was thank you, that would be enough.
—Meister Eckhart

Length of Session:

Time of Day:

Reflect on the following experiences and describe in detail.

What is your intention?

_____
_____

Visual Experience (what were you seeing)

_____
_____
_____
_____
_____

Emotional Experience (what were you feeling)

_____
_____
_____
_____
_____

Mental Experience (what were you thinking)

_____
_____
_____
_____
_____

Physical Experience (what were you sensing)

_____
_____
_____
_____
_____

Final Impressions

_____
_____
_____
_____
_____
_____
_____
_____
_____
_____
_____

MEDITATION SESSION #18

We must find time to stop and thank the people who make a difference in our lives.
—John F. Kennedy

Length of Session:

Time of Day:

Reflect on the following experiences and describe in detail.

What is your intention?

_____
_____

Visual Experience (what were you seeing)

_____
_____
_____
_____
_____

Emotional Experience (what were you feeling)

_____
_____
_____
_____
_____

Mental Experience (what were you thinking)

Physical Experience (what were you sensing)

Final Impressions

MEDITATION SESSION #19

When I started counting my blessings my whole life turned around.
—Willie Nelson

Length of Session:

Time of Day:

Reflect on the following experiences and describe in detail.

What is your intention?

_____

_____

Visual Experience (what were you seeing)

_____

_____

_____

_____

_____

Emotional Experience (what were you feeling)

_____

_____

_____

_____

_____

Mental Experience (what were you thinking)

___

Physical Experience (what were you sensing)

___

Final Impressions

___

MEDITATION SESSION #20

No matter what you are going through, there's a light at the end of the tunnel.
—Demi Lovato

Length of Session:

Time of Day:

Reflect on the following experiences and describe in detail.

What is your intention?
_____
_____

Visual Experience (what were you seeing)
_____
_____
_____
_____
_____

Emotional Experience (what were you feeling)
_____
_____
_____
_____
_____

Mental Experience (what were you thinking)

_____
_____
_____
_____
_____

Physical Experience (what were you sensing)

_____
_____
_____
_____
_____

Final Impressions

_____
_____
_____
_____
_____
_____
_____
_____
_____
_____
_____
_____

MEDITATION SESSION #21

How wonderful it is that nobody need wait a single moment before starting to improve the world.
—Anne Frank

Length of Session:

Time of Day:

Reflect on the following experiences and describe in detail.

What is your intention?

_____

_____

Visual Experience (what were you seeing)

_____

_____

_____

_____

Emotional Experience (what were you feeling)

_____

_____

_____

_____

Mental Experience (what were you thinking)

_____
_____
_____
_____
_____

Physical Experience (what were you sensing)

_____
_____
_____
_____
_____

Final Impressions

_____
_____
_____
_____
_____
_____
_____
_____
_____
_____
_____

References

"10 Mindfulness Exercises for Living in the Present Moment." Mindvalley, January 25, 2019. blog.mindvalley.com/stay-present/.

"101 Best Louise Hay Affirmations of All Time." Louise Hay, June 6, 2018. www.louisehay.com/101-best-louise-hay-positive-affirmations/.

"14 Brain Hacks that Instantly BOOST Your Attention." NJlifehacks. www.njlifehacks.com/instantly-boost-attention-focus/.

"71 Mindfulness Exercises for Living in the Present Moment." Develop Good Habits, December 5, 2018. www.developgoodhabits.com/mindfulness-exercises/#tab-con-1.

Allayer, Samantha. "4 Ways To Master the Art of Patience." Samantha Allaker, March 30, 2018. samanthaallaker.com/4-ways-to-master-the-art-of-patience/.

Babauta, Leo. "15 Tips for Becoming as Patient as Job." Zen Habits, July 6, 2008. zenhabits.net/15-tips-for-becoming-as-patient-as-job/.

Blanchard, Beverly. "The Law of One." Ancient Wisdom, March 30, 2013. beverlyblanchard.blogspot.com/2013/03/the-law-of-one.html.

———. "Law of Projection." Ancient Wisdom, April 16, 2013. beverlyblanchard.blogspot.com/2013/04/law-of-projection.html.

———. "Law of Abundance." Ancient Wisdom, April 21, 2013. beverlyblanchard.blogspot.com/2013/04/law-of-abundance.html.

———. "The Law of Prosperity." Ancient Wisdom, August 27, 2013. beverlyblanchard.blogspot.com/2013/08/the-law-of-prosperity.html.

———. "The Law of Free Will." Ancient Wisdom, July 31, 2016. beverlyblanchard.blogspot.com/2016/07/the-law-of-free-will.html.

———. "The Law of Responsibility." Ancient Wisdom, December 28, 2016. beverlyblanchard.blogspot.com/2016/12/the-law-of-responsibility.html.

———. "The Law of Unconditional Love." Ancient Wisdom, April 25, 2018. beverlyblanchard.blogspot.com/2018/04/the-law-of-unconditional-love.html.

Chidananda, Sri Swami. 1999. *Guidelines to Illumination.* http://www.dlshq.org/download/illumination.htm.

Chopra, Deepak. "5 Steps to Setting Powerful Intentions." The Chopra Center, October 7, 2012. https://chopra.com/articles/5-steps-to-setting-powerful-intentions.

Collins, Keith. "Universal Laws of Perspective." "The Inner Coach," December 19, 2013. www.asktheinnercoach.com/resources/universal-laws-of-perspective.

Fernandez, Elayna. "21 Words to Ban from Your Vocabulary for Good." Elayna Fernandez—The Positive MOM, December 29, 2015. www.thepositivemom.com/21-words-to-ban-from-your-vocabulary-for-good.

Frazer, Jaemin. "A Simple Explanation of the BE DO HAVE Model." Jaemin Frazer, January 10, 2018. https://jaeminfrazer.com/blog/a-simple-explanation-of-the-be-do-have-model.

Griffin, Trudi. "How to Be Emotionally Detached." WikiHow, July 9, 2019. www.wikihow.com/Be-Emotionally-Detached.

Holmes, Lindsay. "5 Tricks to Becoming a More Patient Person." HuffPost, 7 December 7, 2017. www.huffpost.com/entry/patience-tips_n_5843928.

"How to Stop Being Negative: 37 Habits to Stop Negativity Forever." Develop Good Habits, July 22, 2019. www.developgoodhabits.com/how-to-stop-being-negative/.

Jamail, Shannon. "7 Ways to Practice Detachment." Sivana East, April 25, 2018. blog.sivanaspirit.com/7-ways-to-practice-detachment/.

Jennifer. "How to Master Patience—20 Powerful Tips." Contentment Questing, May 1, 2019. contentmentquesting.com/how-to-master-patience/.

Lamb, Cynthia. 2018. *Vibrant Freedom Conscious Healing: Foundational Principles of Awakening.* vibrantfreedom.com/wp-content/uploads/2018/02/ULofAttention.pdf.

"Law of Relativity." n.d. Laws of the Universe. lawsoftheuniverse.weebly.com/law-of-relativity.html.

Paton, Belinda. 2018. *108 Wisdom Principles.* twoworldswisdom.org/downloads/108_Wisdom_Principles.pdf.

Razzetti, Gustavo. "15 Simple Exercises to Increase Your Self-Awareness." Ladders, March 13, 2019. www.theladders.com/career-advice/15-simple-exercises-to-increase-your-self-awareness.

Riordan, Holly. "7 Negative Words to Remove from Your Vocabulary to Be Happier ..." Allwomenstalk, November 13, 2014. inspiration.allwomenstalk.com/negative-words-to-remove-from-your-vocabulary-to-be-happier/.

Robbins, Mike. "Be, Do, Have." Mike Robbins, October 6, 2009. mike-robbins.com/be-do-have/.

Rosemary. "Spiritual Laws—Law of Attachment." Soul Essence, May 17, 2009. https://soul-essence.com/2009/05/17/spiritual-laws-law-of-attachment/

Rubin. "How to Be More Patient: 12 Tips to Master Patience." Happy Rubin, June 17, 2018. happyrubin.com/virtues/patience/.

Salmansohn, Karen. "5 Habits that Stop Negative Thinking." Power of Positivity, April 25, 2019. www.powerofpositivity.com/5-habits-halt-negative-thinking/.

Sicinski, Adam. "Law of Responsibility: What Is?" *MasterMind Matrix*, December 31, 2015. mastermindmatrix.com/knowledge-base/law-of-responsibility/.

"Spiritual Law of Attention." Body and Soul—Mind and Spirit, February 15, 2011. bodysoulmind.net/spiritual-law-of-attention.

Stellman, Justin. "7 Words to Remove from Your Vocabulary." Extreme Health Radio, February 10, 2014. www.extremehealthradio.com/7-words-to-remove-from-your-vocabulary/.

Wagner, Kathryn. "17 Affirmations to Release Negative Thoughts." Spirituality & Health, April 18, 2016. https://spiritualityhealth.com/articles/2016/04/18/17-affirmations-release-negative-thoughts.

Walmsley, Joanne. "The Spiritual Law of PERSPECTIVE." Universal Spiritual Laws, September 21, 2010. universalspirituallaws.blogspot.com/2010/09/spiritual-law-of-perspective.html.

———. "The UNIVERSAL SPIRITUAL LAWS." Universal Spiritual Laws, 2018. universalspirituallaws.blogspot.com/p/universal-spiritual-laws.html.

Williamson, Jennifer. "An Affirmation for Your Negative Thoughts (P.S. They're Not YOU)." Healing Brave, August 14, 2017. aimhappy.com/affirmation-negative-thoughts/.

Young Entrepreneur Council. "12 Ways to Shift Your Mindset and Embrace Change." *Inc.,* April 6, 2015. https://www.inc.com/young-entrepreneur-council/12-ways-to-shift-your-mindset-and-embrace-change.html.

Zaslove, Mira. "3 Powerful Ways to Practice Patience." HuffPost, September 23, 2017. www.huffpost.com/entry/3-powerful-ways-to-practice-patience_b_59c5f0e9e4b08d66155042b2?guccounter=1&guce_referrer=aHR0cHM6Ly93d3cuZ29vZ2xlLmNvbS8&guce_referrer_sig=AQAAANhlWfXMm3l0sFNlTXwqZ8HcztON7XQ_atd8c1vijkPWwMHKe1zkS9lcvMBvamffPO3hLzDbkjIY_B8beWki1VM7Eh54xBs5b7zMa891ss401QvC_KhNJ__3WI3amPwy7vex_BuVw6cOnYQWyREEINGtwNvaiFiS3oP53HeXof8Z.

Bios

Deb Bailey currently lives a quiet life in northern Wisconsin. Her meditation practice has taken her "beyond the veil" for the past thirty years and has been instrumental in bringing clarity to her own life and the lives of others seeking spiritual guidance. As a Reiki master and licensed social worker, Deb has dedicated her professional life to serving others during their times of personal struggle, gaining insights into the human condition and the limitations certain belief systems impose on our lives. Her travel abroad has exposed her to different cultural ideologies and practices while recognizing that all human beings share the same need for love and self-fulfillment. Navigating the path we call life with others is her passion.

Sarah Melland grew up in the small town of Altoona, Wisconsin, and studied creative writing at the University of Wisconsin-Eau Claire. She now resides in Los Angeles, California, where she continuously researches women's issues, relationship faux pas, and dating mishaps. She wants to empower women by sharing the slipups she has experienced throughout her life. Melland is an attuned Reiki master who assists clients in becoming their true authentic selves.

Instagram: @yourdatingunexpert
Facebook: @yourdatingunexpert
Website: www.sarahmelland.com

Email: PracticingLoveBook@gmail.com

www.ingramcontent.com/pod-product-compliance
Lightning Source LLC
Chambersburg PA
CBHW081228080526
44587CB00022B/3864